ADHD

DECODED

A COMPREHENSIVE GUIDE TO ADHD IN ADOLESCENTS

Volume 2

By Leila Molaie

higherself@mobiagroup.com

*To my dear husband and children for their love
and support throughout my life.*

"Why fit in when you were born to stand out?"

— DR. SEUSS

CONTENTS

INTRODUCTION

Welcome to the second volume of this book on ADHD in adolescence. In the first volume, I discussed the signs, symptoms, and treatment options available for ADHD. I highlighted the positive aspects of ADHD, the importance of managing emotions, and how individuals with ADHD can use their unique strengths to their advantage. However, ADHD can still pose significant challenges in many areas of life, particularly in social skills, relationships, and executive function. Knowing this is crucial to building a solid foundation for the topics covered in the second volume.

This book continues from where we previously left off and is a guide to helping adolescents with ADHD navigate the complexities of social skills, relationships, executive function, time management, memory, impulse control, and planning for their future. Adolescents with ADHD can often feel misunderstood and isolated. They may struggle to form and maintain relationships with peers, family, and colleagues. Social skills are essential for building relationships; without them, teenagers with ADHD may experience social exclusion, anxiety, and depression. Therefore, this volume aims to provide practical strategies and tools to help adolescents with ADHD develop social skills and foster meaningful relationships.

Additionally, adolescents with ADHD often struggle with executive function, affecting their ability to manage time, prioritize tasks, and stay organized. These difficulties can significantly impact their academic performance and daily activities. Therefore, this book provides strategies to help young adults with ADHD improve their executive function skills and enhance their academic and personal success.

This volume also addresses other vital areas that can pose challenges for adolescents with ADHD. These include memory, impulse control, and planning for adult life, as they often struggle to remember tasks, instructions, and essential information. They can learn different memory strategies to retain and recall information effectively, deal with impulsive decision-making and behavior, and learn to set goals, plan their future, and make informed decisions. Therefore, this volume offers practical strategies to help teenagers with ADHD improve their impulse control skills. It aims to guide and support young adults with ADHD as they transition from adolescence to adulthood.

Thus, my goal was to begin by introducing ADHD in adolescents, offering a foundation of understanding for readers. As the chapters progress in each volume, the content gradually delves into specific challenges and techniques that become increasingly relevant as individuals with ADHD transition into older age groups. From exploring social dynamics and executive functions to addressing planning, organization, time management, problem-solving, impulse control, and self-advocacy, this comprehensive guide equips readers with valuable insights and strategies tailored to their evolving needs and experiences.

I wanted to take the opportunity to strongly emphasize the importance of parental involvement and professional support in assisting adolescents with ADHD to implement and effectively utilize the discussed techniques. By embracing a collaborative approach and drawing upon the combined efforts of parents, professionals, and individuals, this comprehensive guide aims to empower readers with practical tools for managing ADHD and fostering lifelong success.

Furthermore, the techniques and strategies outlined in this book are not only beneficial for adolescents with ADHD but also hold relevance for adults and individuals of any age who are managing ADHD. Recognizing that ADHD challenges persist into adulthood, the strategies and insights shared in these pages extend their usefulness beyond adolescence, providing valuable guidance for individuals navigating ADHD throughout their lives. By offering practical advice, insights, and approaches, this comprehensive guide aims to support anyone with ADHD in enhancing their daily lives, improving their relationships, and achieving personal and professional success. Whether you're an adolescent, an adult, or someone supporting an individual with ADHD, the tools shared in this book can be invaluable in navigating the unique challenges and harnessing the strengths associated with ADHD at any stage of life.

I aim for this book to serve as a valuable resource for adolescents with ADHD and their families. I believe that with support and practical strategies, adolescents with ADHD can achieve their full potential and thrive in life.

Let us embark on this journey together and help young adults with ADHD develop the skills and tools they need to succeed.

PART I

BUILDING BRIDGES

1

DEVELOPING YOUR SOCIAL NETWORK

We are social beings and constantly interact with others through our relationships, work, or in the community. This makes it necessary to improve our interpersonal skills and make them as effective as possible. These skills play a more critical role for those with ADHD due to their difficulty with impulse control, spontaneity, and emotions.

THE MOST TYPICAL SOCIAL DIFFICULTIES THAT KIDS AND TEENAGERS WITH ADHD DEAL WITH

Trouble Picking Up on Social Cues

Due to ADHD, you may sometimes be unaware of your interactions' impact on others frequently interrupting others and breaking social rules. This can have various consequences, ranging from losing respect to being excluded from social groups. Forming meaningful relationships with peers or making friends can pose challenges because you do not know what is considered socially acceptable or how to act appropriately in different situations. This does not mean you cannot interact socially; you must constantly work on your social skills. Because you may have trouble reading or picking up on social cues, you may not realize that people are uncomfortable. You may not even realize when you hurt someone's feelings, which could lead to misunderstandings, arguments, and conflict. You may also be hyper-focused on one activity (such as a video game), so you easily miss what is happening around you and how your behavior impacts others.

Trouble Keeping Friends

You are often attracted to things that are not conducive to social interaction. Difficulty connecting with others, poor assertiveness skills, and a short attention span can make it difficult to keep friends. Additionally, school-work may overwhelm you, so you might not have time to socialize or enjoy your free time as much as other kids do. As a result, you may refrain from making new friends by isolating yourself or hanging out with the same crowd. You may feel you have to hide your struggles to make friends. This can backfire and make you seem "cold" or "mean." This can be especially problematic when learning how to interact with people because you need to figure out what social rules you are expected to follow in different situations.

You may struggle to fit in with other kids because you may not understand how to act as your peers do. For example, you may joke around when others want to stay serious. You may get distracted during activities that require little movement or be jittery in class while other kids are quiet. You may interrupt other people when they speak or come up with a comment or question when it is inappropriate. You may also need help communicating your thoughts and feelings about different subjects so that others may misinterpret what you genuinely mean. This can lead to feelings of rejection or social isolation.

Going Off-Topic

Remember what you've discussed when you need more time to complete a conversation. You may ask question after question or switch from one subject to another when another person hopes to hear about your daily activities or interests. You can be distracted by unrelated thoughts or problems that enter your mind, making it hard to stay focused on the topic. You may need time to organize your ideas to share something with others. Because of this, other people may find your excessive talk less interesting and may even become bored or annoyed.

Being Inconsistent or Unreliable

You may need help organizing tasks and time. You may forget important things, such as completing projects on time or being at the right place at the right time. Others may judge you for being unreliable or irresponsible when working on group projects, which happens repeatedly. You may also lack the motivation to put energy into your work, making it harder to finish a project successfully. You may have trouble communicating your thoughts to others, so they may not see your potential or creativity. Thus, you may lose many opportunities. Other people might interpret your lack of interest in an activity as disinterest in, or dislike for, those around you, eventually causing unnecessary tension or leading to arguments and fights.

You may also forget to inform people of important dates or events. This can be frustrating for you and forces you to rely on teachers, parents, or other adults to keep you informed about an assignment due date, spelling tests, being on time for a movie, etc.

Overreacting

When you have strong emotions or are surprised, your reactions may be more robust than others expect. For example, in various situations, you might find it challenging to manage your emotions when upset, express joy through loud laughter, or raise your voice when feeling angry. Developing the ability to respond appropriately in different circumstances may be necessary. Your reaction depends on the intensity of your emotions at that moment and how strongly those emotions affect you.

When you feel angry or frustrated about life events, your responses may not make sense to other people or match the situation's intensity. Others may encounter significant challenges when attempting to relate to you, leading to misunderstandings and arguments with others. You may not have the words to explain how you feel, know when you are angry, or get confused when you are tired or bored. Experiencing frustration and struggling to think clearly about your surroundings can lead to significant issues.

You are familiar with these problems, which complicate your social life and make communicating or interacting with others difficult. Taking the time to reflect on your relationships with others and identify improvement areas is crucial. So, how can you improve your social life?

WHAT ARE SOCIAL SKILLS AND COMPETENCIES?

Our ability to interact with others, including friends, partners, adults, and authoritative figures, depends on our social skills. Social competence is the ability to perform well socially in different situations. However, social skills do not develop automatically; we need to learn them through life experiences and interactions. We all have the potential to be socially competent in areas like self-expression, communication, collaboration, leadership, and influence. However, not all individuals can consistently excel in these areas and may still exhibit shortcomings or lack proficiency in one or more of these aspects.

SOCIAL SKILLS TO DEVELOP

So how can you develop social skills to improve your relationships with others? The positive news is that anyone can develop social skills by following appropriate steps and receiving the necessary support. The following are the key areas you need to focus on:

1. Emotional Intelligence

The most important aspect of our everyday social skills is emotional intelligence, which deals with our emotions and how we manage them. You can learn how to manage emotions through self-awareness and awareness of others, which is the ability to identify your feelings while at the same time being aware of other people's feelings. If you can master emotional intelligence, you can focus your energy on the right direction.

2. Communication Skills

Communication is one of the most essential social skills to hone. You can also manage your emotions and express your feelings through your communication. The ideal approach is to be straightforward and honest without crossing the line into rudeness or causing harm. It is preferable to communicate in a calm and clear tone. This includes emotional self-awareness and empathetic listening skills. Developing effective listening skills will enhance your ability to understand and empathize with others, demonstrating your genuine interest in comprehending their perspectives and fostering improved communication.

3. Social Thinking Skills

Social thinking is thinking about how others may experience various situations differently. It is an essential skill because it helps us understand others and recognize their needs and desires. By developing social thinking skills, we can consider how other people may be affected by a specific situation or event, which allows us to respond with empathy and compassion.

You can improve your social thinking skills by identifying your emotions and the feelings of others, understanding how the situation in question may impact other people, and considering how you may appropriately respond when something unexpected happens. To enhance social thinking skills, one of the most effective methods is to ask questions that facilitate a deeper understanding of how others might feel in each situation. You can remain respectful and sensitive to their needs as well. For example, if someone is upset with a teacher, it is essential to recognize their feelings and ask why they are frustrated. You can also ask if they are okay or what they need. The answers help you better understand that person's needs and where they are coming from.

4. Peer/Group Relationships

Peer support is crucial in developing your social skills and can also enhance your relationships with others. This includes learning how to deal with disagreements to maintain social harmony. It will help you practice being non-judgmental and sensitive to another person's feelings while also having the ability to make right decisions. Learning how to deal with disagreements positively will turn into teamwork. A valuable method to practice this is by acquiring the ability to resolve conflicts peacefully and positively, fostering an environment where everyone can collaborate harmoniously.

5. Social Interactions

Social interactions are vital to your relationships with others. Interacting involves being able to follow along with the conversation while at the same time understanding what others are saying without interrupting them. Therefore, it's crucial to refrain from interrupting others when they speak and wait for your turn in a conversation. To develop this skill, it is important not only to contemplate what you wish to say but also to patiently wait for an opportunity in the conversation to voice your thoughts and opinions on a specific topic or issue.

6. Self-Management

Self-management is the ability to control and master your emotions while regulating your attention and staying focused on a task. This helps you make better decisions, and consequently, you can manage your feelings more effectively. One approach is to recognize and acknowledge both your personal emotions and the emotions of others. You can also determine how others are feeling in a specific situation. This allows you to respond appropriately and deal with the issue compassionately instead of taking things too personally.

7. Social Problem-Solving

You can overcome social problems with little to no effort if you can think quickly to solve your social dilemmas. Problem-solving involves creating creative solutions so that there are multiple ways to solve an issue so that everyone benefits. This consists in understanding the problems first before deciding how to handle them, rather than making decisions spontaneously or without considering the possible consequences that come with them. By practicing this, you will acquire a deeper understanding of how to resolve situations in a more effective and productive manner.

8. Interpersonal Relationships

Interpersonal relationships involve understanding yourself and other people well enough to build healthy connections and relate to one another emotionally. When we cultivate healthy relationships, we enhance our self-understanding and develop greater emotional awareness. Interpersonal relationships are vital to your social skills because they enable you to understand yourself better and relate to and communicate with others on an emotional level to maintain positive and meaningful relationships with them.

To put this into practice, focus on fostering friendships that are built on mutual trust and respect rather than solely making decisions based on personal benefit. This approach will enable you to enrich your interpersonal relationships, making them more effective and genuine.

9. Social Influence

Social influence refers to building positive mutual relationships with others by helping them feel comfortable in their current situation. You can also sustain these relationships by helping others recognize the positive aspects of the connection rather than dwelling on negative interactions. Successful people commonly employ this to gain trust and respect in society, be team players, share ideas, and make decisions. One way you can practice social influence is by not just thinking about what you want to say but also waiting for an opening in the conversation so that you can express your thoughts and opinions about a specific topic or issue.

10. Self-Confidence

Self-confidence is essential for succeeding in social situations because it helps you feel calm and grounded around others, allows you to make better decisions based on facts instead of imagination, and, finally, permits you to deal with the outcomes without feeling pressured or overwhelmed by emotions.

You can practice this by identifying your weaknesses and learning the skills you need to grow stronger. You can also use others' suggestions and advice to improve your abilities. For example, if someone gives you advice on communicating more effectively, you can listen and act on it to improve your social life. This is called **internalizing external advice**.

Self-confidence is also an essential part of building trust and a better relationship with yourself. When you build self-confidence, it allows you to feel good about yourself instead of judging yourself negatively.

11. Decision Making

Making firm and accurate decisions is vital to social skills because it helps you stand out among others and function productively when necessary. Your choices are based on logic and reason instead of being influenced by negativity or peer pressure. In practicing this, it is crucial to confidently stand up for your beliefs without compromising, even when facing opposition from others. It is important to stay true to your values and resist external pressures that may lure you into acting against your better judgment.

As you grow socially, you will have more friends and connections with people with the same interests as you do; this will help broaden your social skill set and develop an understanding of other people on a deeper level. It's critical to recognize which socialization aspects are lacking in your abilities and prioritize those areas when forming relationships with others.

THE ROLE OF COMMUNICATION IN SOCIAL SKILLS

Communication is vital to social skills because it empowers you to work alongside others with mutual understanding and without creating conflict or confusion between team members. Additionally, it allows you to learn from your mistakes and resolve any issues. A vital aspect of this is building trust with your partners; if they are open and honest towards you, they will be more likely to accept what you say. You can understand their emotions, thoughts, and feelings instead of just making assumptions.

Developing the skill of engaging in meaningful conversations with others fosters rapport and strengthens connections between individuals. If the situation calls for a more serious response, it is essential, to be honest about your beliefs and show the other person that you are truthful and genuine. Some people use comedy as a coping strategy to handle difficult circumstances. This is the best tactic if it is done at the right time. Being honest and straightforward with others is essential because it creates mutual trust between you and your team.

Social Skills Disorder

The National Institute of Mental Health uses the term "social skills disorder" to refer to individuals who experience challenges with social skills. This can be considered social anxiety because many individuals have trouble making and keeping friends, are often seen as awkward in social settings, and have difficulty approaching strangers. For instance, consider someone who has experienced consistent rejection throughout their life and holds the belief that they are disliked or unwanted by others. If this individual also has ADHD, it can adversely affect their ability to engage in social situations, sustain attention during conversations, and adhere to social norms. Consequently, they may be perceived as socially awkward in social settings.

2

NAVIGATING SOCIAL SKILL CHALLENGES: STRATEGIES FOR BUILDING STRONGER CONNECTIONS

If you have ADHD, there are multiple characteristics that you may exhibit in your relationships, such as being impulsive, disorganized, aggressive, overly sensitive, intense, emotional, or disruptive. Misunderstanding and miscommunication are common in social interactions with others, such as your parents, siblings, teachers, and friends. The ability to self-regulate your actions and reactions toward others is also impaired and, in some cases, can make relationships overly tense and fragile.

ADHD AND THE ACQUISITION OF SOCIAL SKILLS

People may learn social skills through incidental learning, which includes watching people, copying their actions, practicing different behaviors, and receiving feedback. Most people begin this process during their early childhood. The practice and refinement of social skills occur when "playing grown-up" and other childhood activities. Through observation and peer feedback, the finer points of social interactions are sharpened with more practice and become more automatic and habitual.

Due to the challenges associated with impaired attention, hyperactivity, impulsivity, and other related difficulties, individuals with ADHD may find it more challenging to develop social skills than their peers. These symptoms often continue into adulthood, leading to adults with ADHD being observed to have lower social skill levels compared to those without the condition.

Social Skills Research on Children with ADHD

Several studies have discovered that children with ADHD face various social challenges, including disrupted peer relationships, difficulties making friendships and maintaining it, and deficiencies in appropriate social behavior. Long-term outcome studies have found that these difficulties persist into adolescence and adulthood and negatively impact the social adjustment of adults with ADHD.

Social skills training, commonly conducted with groups of children has become a widely accepted treatment modality due to its success. Social skills training groups are typically structured around specific social behaviors targeted by the therapist. The therapist then provides verbal instructions and demonstrations of each target behavior and coaches the children as they role-play the target behaviors. As part of this process, the therapist gives positive feedback and encourages group members to provide positive feedback to one another for exhibiting appropriate social behavior. The children are instructed to use their newly acquired abilities outside the structured group setting in their everyday lives (McGuire, 2022).

Other recent studies have shown that people with ADHD face challenges beyond their lack of appropriate social skills. Children and teens with ADHD tend to face higher levels of peer rejection than children without ADHD. Consequently, this can result in anxiety, diminished self-esteem, and increased social isolation, which are more likely to have negative consequences for individuals with ADHD. Social isolation can also lead to academic difficulties for children with ADHD. Very often, they are found to be academically underachieving, even when they have relatively normal or, at times, higher intelligence, and emotional maturity.

These factors could indicate that ADHD makes it more difficult for people to form meaningful social relationships. Thus, we can conclude that people with ADHD may be less sensitive to the subtle cues that help us understand and predict the behavior of others, or they may struggle to understand how others think and feel, making social interactions more difficult (Brady, 2022).

Specific ADHD Symptoms and Social Skills

Inattention

Inattention has multiple social implications for people with ADHD. Concentrating on a task usually demands the person's full attention. However, those with ADHD struggle to focus on a task or activity. This can be problematic when it reflects a lack of attention to detail. They may overlook details or imperfections in their work that others would automatically notice and attend to.

Another aspect of inattention relates to difficulty connecting the dots and seeing the big picture about what a person is saying or doing. It can be difficult to

ADHD DECODED | 37

grasp the long-term consequences of your decisions or how others may interpret your words and behaviors. In other words, you may tend to believe that others are intentionally behaving in a certain way, even if their actions were unintentional. This lack of insight can gradually result in persistent maladaptive behaviors, such as persisting with a habit despite disappointment from peers (e.g., continuing to act like a superhero despite negative feedback), disregarding the necessary steps to achieve a goal (e.g., making impulsive and inappropriate choices towards reaching an objective), and demonstrating poor judgment (e.g., prioritizing immediate rewards despite requiring more effort or having a lower likelihood of long-term success).

Impulsivity

Because others may attribute impulsive words or actions to a lack of caring or regard for others, impulsivity has a negative impact on social relationships. Failure to pause and consider one's actions can have disastrous social consequences. Impulsivity in speech can appear as unfiltered thoughts if you don't self-edit what you're about to say. Opinions and beliefs are expressed without the usual veneer that most people put on to appear socially acceptable. You may tend to talk more than others, and when you talk, you often use more words than is socially appropriate.

The impulsivity associated with ADHD is not limited to excessive talking but also encompasses a lack of self-control. You may find yourself acting on impulses without considering the consequences or the impact on yourself and others. You may start a task without finishing it properly. This is frequently the case, even if there are negative consequences for not finishing or starting a task correctly. For example, when playing a game, you may act before thinking about your decisions to move your turn along, even though this might cause you to lose the game for everyone.

Impulsivity also has negative social implications because you may always be mentally and physically in overdrive. You may interrupt others' conversations because you talk more or faster than most people.

Hyperactivity

You may demonstrate the symptoms of hyperkinesis (such as rapid movements, blurting out answers to questions, and speaking out before others are finished speaking) and hypokinesis (such as remaining quiet or appearing to lack energy and enthusiasm) even when you are not engaged in a particular activity. Hyperactive children often seem overly enthusiastic about seemingly trivial, poorly coordinated tasks. Consequently, it may be difficult for others to understand what you want from them, and your behavior may appear fragmented or confusing. Being inattentive may seem distracted and disorganized, although you may be able to plan, organize and follow through on tasks. The perceived disorganization stems from inattention and difficulty maintaining focus. However, in the case of hyperactivity, individuals may clearly understand the tasks at hand yet encounter difficulties in organizing their actions due to struggles with self-control.

Additionally, the hyperactivity seen in you may annoy others by being too energetic, intrusive, disruptive, or impulsive. You may be oblivious to the effect of your action on others because you are so caught up in your world and act without thinking. In response to your hyperactivity, some parents may take over by telling you what to do or how to behave. This could be perceived as a parent's attempt to manage or control you to deal more effectively with your impulsivity, inattention, and talkativeness. However, this behavior can result in poor self-esteem since you may feel others should always intervene to help.

Assessment of Social Skills

Interviews and self-report questionnaires are the most common tools for assessing social skill deficits and interpersonal interaction issues. The examiner first asks questions about how others perceive the child during the interviews.

The questions can be categorized into two groups.

1. Interpersonal Functioning Questions

These questions focus on how well the child can relate to others in various situations and with different people, from immediate family members to non-family members. These questions ask about the child's cognition, emotions, and social skills in various areas and their ability to respond appropriately under different circumstances.

Examples include:

- How would you assess your compatibility and rapport with others?
- How would you describe your interaction and social life with others?
- How would you describe your relationships with adults and older people?
- How does your social behavior change around family and friends?
- Can you recall occasions when relationships with others have been complicated for you (e.g., arguments, embarrassing moments)?

- How well do you know the children in school or around you?
- What do you think about involving children in household responsibilities, such as taking care of their toys and other tasks?
- How well do you know children around your neighborhood?
- Do you have close friends at school? (e.g., classmates, best friends, etc.)
- How well do you get along with teachers?
- How often do you experience positive or negative relationships with your teachers?
- To what extent do you relate to adults (e.g., good friends, parents, relatives) compared to how often can you relate to children around you?
- How significantly do emotions, such as anger or fear, influence the dynamics of interpersonal relationships within the household?
- To what degree are you a part of interactions in your immediate environment, and can people around you openly express their emotions?

2. Social Skills Questions

These questions focus on five domains associated with ADHD symptoms: attention and concentration, organization, distractibility and impulsiveness, peer relationships and socializing (in the home), and conflict management (e.g., conflict resolution, dealing with frustration).

Examples include:

- How often do you lose focus when watching TV or talking with family or friends?
- To what extent is your attention easily distracted in school? (e.g., when trying to listen to instructions, etc.)
- Do you often have trouble staying on task (e.g., concentrating on instructions given?)
- Do you experience challenges in managing your thoughts and behavior during social situations?
- Do people around you often get distracted when they talk to you (e.g., talking very quickly in a way you cannot follow), or do you often interrupt people when they are talking?
- To what extent do you have trouble understanding when people tell you about things (e.g., instructions, including other people, etc.)?
- How well do your organizational skills work in school (e.g., how well can teachers teach if they must explain things to you two or three times, how hard is it to keep track of where items are put, etc.)

- How easily can others understand your ideas and plans?

Treatment Strategies

Once the social skill areas that require improvement have been identified, a referral to a therapist or coach familiar with how ADHD affects social skills is highly recommended. Although medication is the most controversial yet commonly used treatment for ADHD, research indicates it can be an effective treatment strategy. ADHD medications can help ease some of the social problems that children with ADHD face by lengthening their attention span, which means they are less likely to get distracted in class, and it can help with social skills. Parents also play a critical role in assisting children with ADHD. In a study by Arain et al., parents who used parent-training programs significantly improved their ADHD children's social skills. Other studies have shown that parent training therapies can reduce externalizing behavior problems as a critical component of the disorder (Arain et al, 2012).

HOW TO MASTER SOCIAL SKILLS

1. Knowledge

You need to understand why you struggle to connect with others in social settings. Understand your daily struggles to stay focused and the need to overcome this challenge to engage and attend to a conversation. Consequently, it is important to gain a deeper understanding of your challenges, learn effective strategies to address them and develop an action plan for personal growth. You should also be aware that your difficulties in social situations may not always come from your actions but from the fact that individuals around you may not understand or empathize with your problem.

2. Attitude

As stated earlier, a positive attitude is essential during any social interaction. It would be best to remain optimistic about your social interactions rather than feeling discouraged, being a victim, or believing that something is wrong with you or that you are awkward. You can be socially comfortable if you acknowledge the issue and have the willpower to face it. However, it is critical to recognize that this is not a straightforward undertaking and can be one of the most demanding obstacles you encounter. Yet, it is crucial to remember that you are not the only one who experiences such emotions, and you have a support network that is invested in your success.

3. Goals

Educating yourself on how to manage social situations, such as discussing appropriate topics of conversation with others, is crucial as it will help you improve self-esteem and confidence. In addition, having clear goals, such as how many social interactions with individuals are needed before the goal of improving one's social skills is reached, will help you organize your day.

4. The Echo

This means repeating things to the person you're speaking with to see if they understand you. This helps you reduce your anxiety and build a better rapport with others. When speaking, both sides are so focused on getting their point across that they often miss the point being made. So, you need to listen actively and look for signs if the other individual wants the conversation to end. It is not enough to only understand someone's questions or statements. Instead, you should be open-minded, attentive, and sensitive to the other person's feelings and emotions. If you do not perceive that the other individual has been paying attention, it may be necessary to repeat what was said to ensure clarity and communication.

5. Observe Others

To enhance your social skills, it is valuable to observe and analyze the social skills of others. By practicing this technique, you can acquire the skills to effectively navigate complex social situations and effectively manage your interactions with others. One minor disadvantage of this strategy is that you may sometimes copy and mimic the actions of another individual too closely, leading to a very unrealistic persona.

6. Visualization

Engage in mental simulations where you envision yourself interacting with another individual and allow the interaction to unfold in your imagination. By being creative and visualizing various scenarios, you can effectively plan and strive for the most favorable outcome in your interactions.

7. Role-Play

A perfect technique is role-playing. You can imagine possible scenarios and rehearse interactions in your mind in advance. Role-playing social situations can help you to overcome your anxiety, be well prepared, and reduce possible mistakes without forgetting what needs to be covered.

8. Prompts

Prompts are a simple yet effective tool to increase participation in social situations and help you overcome your shyness. You can use prompts to ask for help, make congratulatory statements, small talk, and much more. One way to practice is by engaging in self-dialogue while looking in the mirror or jotting down sentences you can use in future conversations. The difference between these prompts and simple reminders is that you must deliver them to prompt another individual during a conversation. It is important to note that prompts should be presented in advance to avoid awkward situations.

9. Increase "Likeability"

The significance of likability is often underestimated, yet it plays a crucial role in establishing meaningful connections with others. Building a genuine and positive relationship with another person can have many benefits. It goes beyond physical appearances, such as styling hair or adopting traits commonly perceived as attractive or popular.

Likability encompasses qualities that contribute to being genuinely appealing and relatable to others. It involves demonstrating kindness, empathy, respect, and a sincere desire to comprehend and connect with individuals on a deeper level. By cultivating these qualities, you create an environment of trust, acceptance, and mutual understanding, which forms the foundation of strong relationships.

This can also create a foundation for enriching experiences, personal growth, and a network of individuals who appreciate and value you for who you are.

HOW TO BE A GREAT COMMUNICATOR

1. Pause when Talking

It seems counterintuitive, but often, the little things we do have the most significant influence on how others see us. When speaking, most people are not listening to what we are saying; they look at our facial and physical expressions to figure out when it's their turn to talk. Pausing more between sentences and paragraphs allows those around you with an opportunity to keep pace and prevents them from feeling hurried when it's their turn to express themselves.

2. Listen and Hear

When others speak, refrain from mentally preparing your response and instead focus on listening to them. Avoid rehearsing what you want to say until they have finished expressing their thoughts. Simply dedicate your attention to comprehending their message and verifying if they have additional points to contribute. Once they have completed their statement, reiterate what you understood from their words and inquire if your understanding aligns with their intended meaning.

3. Redirect Your Thoughts to the Newly Defined (and Typically Narrower) Topic

As you listen to the other person, make sure you remain focused on the topic at hand. This can be difficult because you may think about many things simultaneously and get distracted by outside stimuli. The following sentence can make it easier for others to talk to you and for you to concentrate on what they say. Depending on the topic, you can say, **"That's a great idea; where were you going with it?"**

4. Condense Your Answer

After you've listened to the other person, processed what they've said, and returned the conversation's focus to them, it's time to narrow down your response from all your thoughts and be precise. During this process, it is crucial to begin with, open-ended questions such as **"What do you mean by that?"** or **"Let me stop you and see if I understand your point."** Tell them so if they say something that doesn't make sense or isn't true. Tell them why you think as you do if they disagree with what you said.

HOW TO LISTEN ATTENTIVELY

1. Try to Understand First

Maintaining clear communication is crucial in ensuring mutual understanding. To facilitate two-way conversations, it is essential to actively listen without interrupting the other person. However, if interruption becomes necessary, apologize, and express your intention to contribute to the discussion without causing disruption. Convey your point clearly and allow the other person to continue expressing their thoughts.

For example:

Before making a point, ask the other person if they have a clear understanding of your previous point. This can be very helpful in a conversation. Doing this may be more time-consuming at first, but it prevents you from explaining yourself later when the topic changes. If possible, paraphrase what the other person just said as soon as possible after they say it. By employing this approach, you can effectively gather your thoughts and minimize potential confusion.

ADHD DECODED | 51

2. Ask Clarifying Questions

You may need to fully understand the other person's central point during a conversation. An easy way to get clarification is to ask specific questions as they go on.

For example:

"So, what did you mean by that?"

To gain a deeper understanding of the point, it is valuable to ask relevant questions that can provide you with more information.

For example:

"Come again?" or **"That sounded like you were getting at something else."** Engaging in this practice is an excellent method to revisit and clarify the main points of a conversation, thereby reducing the likelihood of misunderstanding. Additionally, asking the other person to restate their main point to ensure a thorough comprehension can be helpful. This approach is particularly advantageous when seeking clarity on complex subjects, as it encourages the speaker to explain more explicitly. Instead of commenting on isolated situations that may require clarification, it is best to focus only on seeking further understanding by asking for clarity once more. **"If I hear you correctly, what you are saying is..."**

If someone diverts the conversation for one reason or another, continue asking questions as long as they are still thinking about the original topic. You can draw the conversation back to its primary point by asking what was said before. Adopting a positive approach when engaging in this practice is typically recommended.

For example:

"I see you clearly understand why that should be the case; now, let's talk about how you will do it." This will demonstrate your interest in the conversation's success.

3. Be Curious

Demonstrating curiosity and genuine interest in the ideas of others is a valuable approach to active listening and engaging in a conversation. By embracing this technique, you can reduce the potential distraction of scattered thoughts and stay focused on the discussion. When you exhibit genuine curiosity toward someone or a particular topic, it becomes challenging to disengage from the interaction. This behavior creates a comfortable environment for the other person to express themselves and fosters higher-quality conversations.

4. It's Okay to Interrupt Sometimes

Often, individuals will continue speaking without pausing. It's okay to interrupt and ask someone to clarify something before they go any further if you're unsure of what they're saying and need clarification.

For example:

"Excuse me! I'm sorry to interrupt, but I wasn't sure I understood what you just said." or "I'm sorry to interrupt, but I need to understand you correctly. Are you saying..." This technique is very helpful, particularly when the other person requires additional time to articulate their thoughts. In addition to helping others express their points clearly, active listening promotes a shared understanding among all partici-pants, reducing confusion in the conversation.

Furthermore, it is beneficial to establish a respectful approach to interjecting or asking questions. By seeking permission from the speaker before speaking, you demonstrate consideration and prevent catching them off guard. This approach fosters a collaborative and harmonious environment where everyone feels valued and heard. **You can do so by prefacing your question with a polite statement like, "I'm sorry to interrupt!"** before proceeding with your inquiry.

5. Take the Time You Need to Think

It may be essential to pause and reflect on what you want to express or what someone has conveyed. This is particularly important when acquiring new knowledge or seeking clarification on an explanation. Taking this pause demonstrates attentive listening and conveys that you are carefully considering the information.

For example:

If someone explains something that needs clarification, be honest and ask questions until it makes sense. If someone starts talking about something new before you can reply, it's okay to say, **"I'm sorry, I need a moment."**

This practice enables you to gather your thoughts; you should know that others will be receptive to this approach. They will understand and accommodate if it takes you longer than usual to comprehend or process information.

COMMUNICATION HACKS

Here are some suggestions to assist with certain communication issues.

1. Forgetfulness

Due to short attention spans and distractibility, it is common for people with ADHD to forget simple things, which may irritate others.

Solution:

1. Pay your full attention and listen attentively to others until they have finished speaking. Minimize distractions by silencing your phone and keeping it out of sight.
2. Jot down notes whenever you need to remember something. If you're writing a reminder, use "TO DO" as the subject line so it gets your attention when you sort through emails.
3. Keep track of important meetings and things to remember using to-do lists or calendars.

2. Talking Too Much

Perhaps you tend to dominate the conversation, especially if you are enthusiastic about the subject. You're probably unaware that you're turning the conversation into a monologue, which can irritate those around you.

Solution:

1. Understand that everyone is different, and work with them instead of arguing about your differences.
2. When you get excited or talk too much in a conversation, seek balance. You can achieve this by asking the person you're speaking with if they'd like to take the conversation further. This approach allows individuals to withdraw from or join the conversation according to their preferred level of comfort. It's vital to avoid interrupting someone else's thought process, as it can discourage them and even lead to misunderstandings.

3. Interrupting

This is a common ADHD-related issue and can be overcome by following the golden rule of conversations: listen first, then speak. The individual you interact with will highly value your attentive listening before sharing your ideas. It can be aggravating when someone interrupts a conversation without genuinely listening to what has been expressed and without taking the time to formulate a response thoughtfully. Demonstrating patience and actively listening, you convey respect and consideration, fostering a more harmonious and productive dialogue.

Solution:

Occasionally, individuals tend to interrupt before fully hearing what is being said. If you find yourself doing so, consciously pause, listen attentively, and avoid jumping into the conversation prematurely. Set limits on the frequency of interruptions made in each period. In addition, there are several things to consider:

- If you feel overwhelmed during a conversation, take a deep breath, and fully exhale.
- Practice not interrupting in your head.
- Admit it if you find yourself interrupting. **"I apologize for interrupting. I want to ensure that I grasp your point correctly."**
- Pay attention to the nonverbal cues of the person you are conversing with, such as facial expressions and body language, as they provide valuable insights into their thoughts and feelings.
- Take a moment to contemplate the speaker's message before formulating your response,

enabling more thoughtful and meaningful contributions to the conversation.

4. Struggle to Find the Right Words

You may have trouble in articulating your thoughts despite knowing what you want to say. Retrieving the precise words from your mind's filing system can be challenging, potentially resulting in using the wrong words. This can lead to misunderstandings, confusion, and the conversation veering off track.

Solution:

1. You may struggle to express yourself even when you know what you're trying to say. Don't stress about this; don't let the other person stop you from getting your point across.
2. If you're stuck on a particular phrase or word, let it go and move on.
3. Suppose you have the opportunity and believe that the other person can continue the conversation later. In that case, it is better to communicate what went wrong instead of forcing yourself to express something on the spot that doesn't effectively convey your message.

5. Going Off-Topic

Going off-topic is not only for individuals with ADHD but for everyone at some point. It is common to get absorbed in the present moment and unintentionally shift the conversation to a different subject. This shift doesn't necessarily require conscious effort; it can happen spontaneously.

Solution:

Adapting and flowing with the conversation is beneficial to avoid frequent off-topic discussions. While it is not ideal to veer off-topic consistently, it is acceptable to transition between different subjects if the conversation remains engaging and coherent. If the need arises to steer the discussion back on track, it is appropriate to gently guide it by saying phrases like, "Let's keep this on the topic" or "I'll let you get back on topic. I'm interested in hearing your thoughts." This approach ensures clarity and facilitates a more focused exchange of ideas.

6. Zoning Out

You can easily become distracted and unintentionally stop listening. Even a brief lapse in your attention during a conversation can result in missing vital information or the main point being discussed. When you become distracted and stop listening, it can create the perception that you are uninterested or deliberately not paying attention to others.

Solution:

1. Maintain eye contact. If you're in a group, make eye contact with others and talk to them to help keep your mind off what isn't important.
2. Instead of allowing your mind to drift, direct your gaze toward the person you are conversing with.
3. If you find your attention waning, recharge your focus by taking brief mental breaks as needed. Taking a breath or a quick walk can help recenter you.

7. Fidgeting

Fidgeting can cause unnecessary disruptions. You may interrupt yourself with unnecessary movements while engaging in other activities, such as typing or checking your phone.

Solution: When confronted with fidgeting tendencies during a conversation, try incorporating grounding techniques. For example, reaching for a pen or stationary object can help redirect your focus and minimize distractions. Taking a deep breath and exhaling while consciously centering your attention on the ongoing discussion can foster a sense of calm and attentiveness. Don't hesitate to request a brief break to gather your thoughts or realign your focus if necessary.

Remember, it is not impolite but rather a way to ensure the conversation remains on track and conducive to effective communication.

3

DELVING DEEP INTO SOCIAL SKILL CHALLENGES

I n addition to medication, therapy, and the previously mentioned tips, there are additional strategies you can employ to enhance your social interactions.

DETERMINE THE ROOT CAUSE OF SOCIAL SHORTCOMINGS AND PRACTICE EFFECTIVE HACKS.

Before jumping into the solutions, determining the root cause of social issues may be a good idea. What causes the most disruption? Do you struggle with sharing, managing emotions, interacting with others, handling excitement, or being flexible? Things like procrastination, likeability, or self-defeating thoughts can be potential causes of social issues. Remember that everyone has their way of thinking, understanding the world, and approaching problems.

Investing time in understanding the underlying causes of your social issues increases your chances of finding effective solutions. Once identified, practicing, and implementing specific strategies and actions to enhance your social interactions is crucial.

Build up Skills (with Parents, Siblings, or Close Friends)

If you've figured out your weakness or hold-up in social situations, you can practice it with people who are good at it. This can improve your social skills and help you become the most well-rounded person you want to be. Remember, practice makes perfect. Your parents or family members are a good resource for you. Combining experience and passion to support you in every step can significantly contribute to building a strong and reliable support network. They can answer your questions about social interaction and guide you on what is socially acceptable in certain situations. Choosing the right individuals to join your circle is life-changing, as they will be consistently invested in teaching, guiding, and offering valuable feedback to help you thrive and excel in life.

You can do this:

1. If you have siblings around your age, you can engage in a game of Truth or Dare. This enjoyable activity serves to get to know each other better and break the initial awkwardness. If you prefer a more collective experience, you can participate in a group setting, making it even more captivating.

2. Arrange outings with your siblings or close friends to enjoy some ice cream while discussing the things that trouble or intrigue you throughout the week. Additionally, take the opportunity to inquire about their daily obstacles and challenges. This fosters a reciprocal connection where both parties genuinely care for and attentively listen to one another. Moreover, it cultivates awareness of your environment and provides a platform to refine your social skills.

3. Ask your parents what they prefer to do if their work requires them to interact with people (e.g., a job interview). Do your best to gain as much knowledge as possible about emotions, body language, etc.

4. Play a game of charades and act out social situations you want to be comfortable in.

5. Do role-play exercises on how to talk to people who are intimidating or make you uncomfortable in the workplace or school (e.g., a phone interview).
6. While watching videos on YouTube, count the times you play them from the beginning until the end without skipping anything or pausing, and then do it with another video (e.g., teaching/video about social skills).
7. Watch videos or read articles on how people with social anxiety handle a social situation.
8. If you have the time, interview, or role-play with someone good at socializing and ask them questions about your most significant limitation (e.g., feeling awkward when making eye contact, being nervous or anxious when talking).

Assign Yourself a Mission (Challenge Yourself)

Envision the goals you wish to accomplish in social situations and establish a mission that is both attainable and desirable. Start by practicing a simple task so you can work on your weakness and work your way up to more important missions.

As a starting point, if you fear speaking in front of groups, consider practicing with a close friend or family members before gradually progressing to larger audiences. Treat your most significant limitations as goals and break them down into smaller tasks, e.g., "I want to talk more to my friends."

Once you've practiced this simple task, move on from it and start looking at more complex skills like eye contact and finding common ground with the person. Once these more manageable tasks are mastered, set out your next mission to complete; this should be much more difficult than the previous ones so that it will push your social skills further. Keep going until you've mastered these strategies by taking on more challenging missions. Remember that socializing goes beyond mere laughter or capturing moments in photographs. It involves forming connections with individuals who may be different from you and ensuring that the interaction holds significance for both participants.

Find Compatible Friends

If your social life primarily revolves around making friends, seeking out like-minded individuals with similar interests might be worthwhile. By finding compatible friends, you can enhance the enjoyment and fulfillment of your social interactions. Connecting with people with shared interests can help overcome any obstacles or apprehensions about forming new friendships. These friends can also become resources for you as they may know some helpful tips and advice that are useful for you. Don't worry too much about having a larger circle of friends; having close, genuine friendships is more important than the number of friends you have.

Observe and Interact More

When you're in a social situation, interact more with people. Don't stand on the sidelines or watch the interaction from a distance; join in and participate in conversation as much as possible. If it's challenging to think of what to say, ask about their life before expressing your opinions. Just say something nice that is relevant or interesting to them, that is all.

Social Skills Exercise: "I Say, You Say"

Practicing this exercise will enhance your understanding that conversations are a two-way street, highlighting the importance of avoiding interruptions, monologues, or raising your voice, as these behaviors hinder meaningful dialogue. Get in the habit of adding to or expanding on a topic. Every conversation has three distinct parts: speaking, listening, and formulating a response. You can switch between talking, listening, and responding in a conversation without any restrictions.

ENGAGING ICEBREAKERS: WHAT YOU CAN SAY TO START MEANINGFUL CONVERSATIONS

1. Ask questions.

Showing curiosity and interest in what others say is a positive quality that will set you apart. The rule of thumb is to be ready to ask questions once the other person has finished speaking; By actively listening to others, you demonstrate your interest in their words, allowing you to raise your point or ask a question once they have finished speaking. It will also help the other person speak and make them feel good about the conversation.

Start your conversation with **"Hello. How are you?"** Try not to be over-expressive with your feelings or use exclamation points. Your goal is to create a positive and lively atmosphere for the other person. It's perfectly fine to smile or nod if you're unsure how to respond in a conversation, but don't force yourself to be someone you're not. Stay attentive and avoid veering off-topic by discussing unrelated matters.

"I have a question" or **"I have an idea"** is an opening for when you don't know what to say in a conversation. This helps you connect with people and find out about their lives. Usually, one person will speak first, but you can still jump in anytime. The point is to be patient to talk and listen when appropriate. You're supposed to ask questions so that they can respond and ask questions too, which will help maintain the flow of the conversation.

2. Delve into the Other Person's World

Learning something new about the other person shows your openness to others, which most people like. You can ask questions about what they've been up to lately or what they think about news, a story, or an event. Bring up an opinion of your own and then listen to their honest opinion. If you demonstrate an interest in who they are and their interests, people will be more receptive and willing to speak with you.

"How are things going today?" or, only after getting to know the other person, **"What have you been up to?"** These open-ended inquiries will elicit a conversation, which is what everyone seeks.

3. Discover Shared Experiences: Ask About Their Interests and Forge Connections.

Ask about their interests. Perhaps you both enjoy a specific restaurant or have a favorite teacher in common. They might share your passion for fishing or summer beach trips. If you find common ground, ask them if they've had any recent experiences or activities they can share with you, and vice versa. This will boost their self-esteem and deepen their understanding of each other.

"Do you like (a teacher, a situation, an activity, a video game)?" or **"I heard so and so likes (a teacher, a situation, an activity, a video game), do you?"** to get the ball rolling. To keep the conversation going and learn something new about someone else, ask how they like what you like. You'll also introduce yourself to your friends and possibly someone new, which is a win-win situation for everyone.

If you see that there is something in common between you and them, comment on it by saying something like, **"That's funny, because I was thinking that..."** or **"Wow, that's interesting, because I was just thinking of..."** giving them the first opportunity to make the connection.

"What do you think?" or **"I don't know if you can do (a task), but "I'm curious to hear your thoughts on what I just mentioned. How would you rephrase it or add to it?"** Everyone has an opinion and needs to be heard. Don't be arrogant or look down on them for not being good at something if you say something. Give them a chance to explain themselves and explain why they can't do something. You'll discover valuable insights about people and their perspectives by actively listening to their responses and encouraging reciprocal questioning. This demonstrates your genuine care for them and their opinions.

4. Engage in Dialogue: Reflecting on the Statement and Posing a Question.

You can say something like, **"That sounds interesting"** or **"That makes sense."** These responses show that you pay attention to the other person, which is vital in any conversation. If you need clarification about something, you can also ask. If you believe something is true, say, **"I think (name subject) is/is not a big deal."** You're telling the person that they have good or bad thoughts about something, but you disagree with them.

"Do you think this is true?" or **"Do you think that is true?"** Ask questions if they seem unsure of themselves in certain situations. If they say that a specific teacher doesn't give homework, ask if they would rather have someone else teach the lesson (if so, ask who it would be) or prefer to have an assignment over the next few weeks.

UNDERSTAND THE GIVE-AND-TAKE OF CONVERSATION AND POSING THOUGHTFUL QUESTIONS

The dynamics of conversation can be intricate, with one person speaking, then the other, and sometimes both talking simultaneously. It may appear straightforward, but many people feel overwhelmed or unsure of what to say when they sense the other person's anticipation for their response. However, in one-on-one conversations, it's beneficial to return to asking questions about shared interests once you've discussed a topic to completion. You can maintain engagement by keeping the subject consistent and inquiring about related aspects. Acknowledging and appreciating humor or exciting contributions from others is important to foster a lively exchange. Additionally, when others join the conversation, understanding the give-and-take dynamics helps you navigate interruptions or surprises smoothly. Although initial nerves are common, practice will build your confidence over time.

In difficult situations, and when the other person continues interrupting you, acknowledge them by saying something like, "**I was listening while you spoke**," showing them that you expect the same while you speak. Conversations should be fluid and natural, not rigid, controlled, or stagnant. Use your intuition and the techniques described in this book to remember what to say next in a conversation. Remember that paying attention to the other person is essential to have a fluid conversation with them.

MORE STRATEGIES

You'll find some excellent tips for maintaining a conversation in this section. You can use techniques you are more comfortable with or find more valuable according to the context.

1. Use your common sense.

Start with small talk if you have difficulty thinking of something to say. Ask the other person about their day, what they had for breakfast, or school that day, as these questions can lead to more exciting dialogue and more personal stories about the other person.

2. Start with a compliment.

To initiate a conversation and make the other person feel important, say something like, "**That looks nice on you / I like that shirt.**" This strategy also works well when feeling more confident. You can extend this compliment by explaining further.

3. Use a compliment to ask a question.

This strategy is identical to the earlier one, but rather than asking a question, you can state, "**That looks nice on you,**" followed by a comment such as "**What is your favorite color?**" The compliments will naturally lead to small talk about how well the other person looks and what they've been doing lately. This strategy is perfect for when you have nothing to talk about because it will make people feel good about themselves, making them more likely to carry on the conversation.

4. Don't talk about yourself.

Redirect the attention to the other person and ensure that the topic is comfortable for them. Ask them what they did the last time they were in the exact location as you, how their day was at work or school last week, or something else interesting if you are having trouble coming up with conversation starters. You'll then be able to ask more personal questions and make small talk.

5. Try to have fun.

Cultivating friendships during adolescence can be difficult for anyone, particularly those with ADHD. Cliques are challenging, and a lack of maturity hampers social success. You can make a joke, laugh, or tell an exciting story if you are not offensive to others. It is vital to be yourself. While some hyperactive, impulsive ADHD teenagers make friends through their enthusiasm and offbeat humor, others are shunned by their peers, who perceive them as overbearing or immature. Any social gathering can be a challenge, paralyzing you into silence. You can't structure your social life as you did in elementary and middle school, but you can give yourself the little push you need to improve your social skills.

The following are examples of "jump starts":

1. School Clubs

Joining any organized activity is a great way to make new friends. Many high schools have career clubs, book clubs, photography clubs, religious groups, etc. If your high school doesn't have the kind of club, you'd like to be in, talk to teachers or friends at other schools, join your community center, or start your club with friends who share your interests. To find the right place for you, visit your high school guidance office or call a community center and ask about youth services. Apply the skills you have learned before. Keep being true to who you are at all times. Do not pretend you are not looking for a friend if you are.

2. Youth Groups

Many cities and towns have organizations that sponsor teen activities and workshops. Youth groups keep you busy and on task and give you a place to belong. Whether sport, music, theater, dance, or visual arts is your thing, these groups offer the chance to meet people who share your interests and develop creative skills while having fun. As someone with ADHD, you have a unique gift to offer, you could make a great leader, and your peers will benefit from your involvement. Know your strengths, and then use them to your advantage. By doing so, you can build and expand a stronger social network.

Youth groups are excellent opportunities for you to:

- Learn to accept responsibilities and be responsible.
- Learn to get along with people in a setting other than school.
- Improve your grades by being punctual and keeping up with deadlines.
- Find someplace where you feel you belong.
- Learn to follow directions and take turns.
- Improve your public speaking skills.
- Find people who share similar interests in things as you.

- Research to get answers to questions concerning your future.

Getting involved with a small group of friends means fewer distractions. When you engage in conversations with a small group of individuals, the focus tends to remain on the topic at hand for a longer duration. This creates an environment conducive to more meaningful discussions as there are fewer distractions. Your keen attention to detail and ability to identify areas for improvement make you an engaging conversationalist, attracting the interest of others. This presents an opportunity to extend your support and assistance to those around you.

3. Outings with Your Parents

Include your parents in your social life by inviting them to events like your high school play or a sporting event. By involving them, they will better understand who you are, your interests, and your abilities. Furthermore, it presents an opportunity to expand your social circle and lead to the formation of new friendships, adding an extra layer of excitement to your social life.

4. Part-Time Jobs

Working after school, on weekends, or during summer is a great way to meet people. You have something in common when you work with others: your job. You can also make friends by having lunch or shopping together during breaks and working with others gives you a chance to learn how to be more responsible and work as part of a team. Additionally, completing things on time will keep you from procrastinating and missing opportunities for new friendships. If you ignore responsibilities and follow-up activities, your social circle may eventually shrink because people around you will see they cannot depend on you.

5. Social-Skill Groups

Learning social skills is a lifelong process. If you have social phobias, try joining a group, or seek help from a professional. A certified school psychologist can direct you to any available resources in your community. Sometimes joining a group can be an effective way to practice the skills you've learned and receive feedback from people who have gone through similar experiences.

ADHD can be quite a challenge to a person's emotional well-being. You may feel frustrated, angry, or upset about your condition. But remember that this does not mean there is something wrong with you. You are strong. You got this.

4

RE-BONDING WITH YOUR LOVED ONES

A DHD can significantly impact adolescent relationships—with peers, parents, siblings, extended family members, and romantic partners. You may often experience excessive frustration and anger due to inattention, disorganization, and procrastination.

UNDERSTANDING THE DYNAMICS

A. ADHD'S EFFECT ON RELATIONSHIPS WITH PARENTS

Below are some factors that can potentially strain your relationship with your parents:

- You may think you're old enough to do something, whereas your parents feel the opposite.
- The symptoms of ADHD increase, making it harder for your parents to understand and manage the problem. You may also worry more about not getting attention at home or being controlled too much.
- As a teen, you naturally turn to your friends for advice and comfort, which is only sometimes helpful and doesn't usually solve anything.
- Parents primarily worry about their children getting into trouble in dangerous neighborhood.
- You have different expectations of what counts as fun than parents (i.e., staying out late, spending too much money, etc.)
- You might not want to seek therapy because you believe it is "uncool" or puts you in a

ADHD DECODED | 83

negative light in society.

- You may be more self-centered–you're on social media apps all the time and on your phone—which is normal for you, but sometimes parents might feel left out or that their authority is undermined.

You might experience challenges in your relationship with your parents due to the following reasons:

1. Disagreement with rules: You may find it difficult to adhere to certain rules, such as curfews, chores, or early wake-up times, as you may question their relevance or significance.
2. Emotional well-being: Research suggests that adolescents commonly face higher levels of depression and anxiety compared to their parents. This can be influenced by internalizing the belief that your parents no longer love you (McGuire, 2022).

It's important to remember that these factors can impact your relationship, but open communication, understanding, and seeking support can help address these issues and improve your connection with your parents.

Ways to Tackle This

1. Treat It as a Partnership

You and your parents should work as a team and plan tasks together. You can't constantly depend on them to do things for you. It would be best to accept responsibilities such as doing homework, making, and keeping appointments, getting to bed at a reasonable hour, doing chores around the house, and setting priorities. Collaboration between you and your parents is essential in determining what is realistic for you. For example, suppose you want a later curfew on Friday night but know you cannot manage it independently and may fall asleep at a friend's house by 10:00 p.m. (or earlier). In such situations, it might benefit you and your parents to mutually agree on an earlier curfew for those nights.

2. Learn to Communicate with Your Parents

Communicating effectively is the key to resolving many conflicts between you and your parents. Because so many symptoms, such as inattention, hyperactivity, impulsivity, moodiness, and poor self-control, are linked with a lack of organization and poor planning, you might find it easier to focus on this area of communication. You may need to help articulate what they need or want you to accomplish. However, you should recognize that your parents have strengths and weaknesses in managing family situations. This realization allows you to respect your parents' strengths while acknowledging their limitations. You might come to understand and value your parents' seemingly arbitrary rules regarding what is allowed or prohibited, as they often stem from genuine safety concerns. Still, they can also be related to their unique upbringing. Your parents can't always anticipate what might happen a day, month, or year in advance.

Not all teenagers view adolescence solely as going out, having fun, and getting their way. Everyone's experience is different, and some teenagers have different priorities and perspectives. People are the most vulnerable between the ages of thirteen and nineteen, which can be scary. Parents may not share your joy at becoming an adult, but that shouldn't turn you against them. Recognizing that your parents are also going through an important phase in their lives and making decisions based on their well-being can help foster understanding and empathy between you and them.

3. Schedule Your Time and Stick With it

Developing a daily schedule that includes all your activities is essential to avoid conflict in your relationship with your parents. You and your parents can work on this together, monitoring how many responsibilities you can handle each day. As you grow older, you can assume additional responsibilities at home, gradually becoming more independent in the process.

4. Transform Your Behavior by Releasing Your Anger

Defiant, temperamental children may become angry and resentful adults when they cannot have their way. Figure out how to express your dissatisfaction without getting into more trouble or convincing yourself that your parents are being unreasonable. It's important to understand why your parents behave as they do so that you can talk with them about appropriate ways of behaving, through which both of you can express negative emotions without getting upset. You should work on learning to talk about this issue so that it does not lead to conflict between you and your parents.

B. THE CONNECTION BETWEEN CHILDREN AND TEENS WITH ADHD AND THEIR SIBLINGS AND EXTENDED FAMILY

- Siblings may believe you receive all the attention and resent that they are subjected to different rules.

- Your siblings may feel like you're stealing your parent's attention and that your parents favor you a lot.
- You should be more considerate of the siblings' personal space.
- You may struggle to 'put the brakes on.'
- If you are in a feud, you may argue with your siblings and provoke them to fight.
- You may have trouble supporting your siblings where needed; thus, you are too caught up in your problems.
- It can be very unfair for your sibling to be blamed for something you did, yelled at, or punished when they had nothing to do with the situation.
- Other relatives might criticize your actions outside the home, doubt that your challenges are unintentional, or not fully acknowledge your efforts.
- Siblings think they are expected to grow up much faster because they must take on more adult responsibilities, and the parents don't expect you the same.

Ways to Tackle This:

1. Try to appreciate the challenges you face.

Taking on an equal relationship with your siblings and other family members is more challenging than you are used to. However, the benefits will be enormous if you can pull it off. Give up your expectations that you should live like an adult—and accept that you are dependent on your parents for financial support and a roof over your head—but join in doing whatever chores you can. This will significantly simplify life for the whole family.

2. Be honest and open with your siblings.

Giving an honest accounting of your problems is the best way to make family issues—which may have been hidden and unreported to you—either improve or worsen. Begin by talking directly to yourself about what is happening without blaming others. If you can get a consensus from your family, everybody will be on the same page about what has to be accomplished.

3. Embrace Imperfection and Discover Its Benefits

Avoid comparing yourself with your siblings, who may not struggle as much as you at school, at home, or outside the home. Accept that those advantages are not within your or your parents and family's reach.

4. Solve problems before they escalate.

Avoid situations that might lead to conflict and make decisions or choices with a risk of being wrong. Be ready to compromise on solutions that both sides can agree with, even if this means leaving things as they are. The goal might be a compromise that holds up under only moderate pressure, but its chances go down if you try to hold out for a more significant solution.

5. Learn to take advantage of your strengths and your weaknesses.

Your strong points are essential and will be utilized in ways you never imagined to help you have a better relationship with your siblings and other family members. If you can accept your family's expectations for how you should behave, you can manage them more effectively than if you always let them get the best of you. The key is avoiding conflict with them and not allowing them to exploit your vulnerabilities.

C. IMPACT OF ADHD ON PERSONAL RELATIONSHIPS

- Coping with the stress of intimate relationships can be challenging, making initiating, sustaining, or nurturing a relationship difficult.

- You may be perceived as self-centered and inconsiderate of others' feelings because you seem insensitive to how your behavior affects others around you.
- You may not connect with your friend, significant other, or partner as you once did, or the relationship may be less intimate than you would like.
- Sometimes, striking a balance between the long-term committed relationship you desire and the need for personal privacy and freedom can be challenging. This challenge may arise from a desire to maintain the independence and autonomy you enjoyed during childhood. You might feel restricted or controlled by your partner, preventing you from engaging in important activities or pursuing your interests.

Ways to Tackle This:

1. Develop a sense of appreciation for the positive aspects of your life.

This can greatly contribute to your overall happiness and enhance your role as a partner or friend. By cultivating gratitude for the good things in your life, you can avoid becoming consumed by minor annoyances. During times of frustration or anger towards your partner or friends, it's common to fixate on trivial matters that bother us, causing us to lose sight of what truly matters. By shifting your focus towards gratitude, you can maintain perspective and prioritize what is truly important.

2. Understand and trust your instincts about your needs.

If you can express what's on your mind, they will understand the problem better. Feel free to express your needs to your partner or friends and kindly ask them to actively listen without interruption when you speak. It's common for couples to experience similar things in the relationship, which might cause communication difficulties.

3. Learn to forgive.

Expecting to live a life free of problems is unrealistic. People make mistakes, and sometimes each person in a relationship is the cause of those problems. If you learn to let those things go, you can have a healthy relationship. Forgiveness is the key.

4. Remember that your partner or friend may not have ADHD.

You might be projecting your emotions and behaviors onto them when they are just thoughtful and considerate. It's easy for someone who is used to being independent to interpret actions that others take in ways that reflect their feelings. It's pointless to be upset about someone's actions if you can't see things from their point of view or comprehend their motives.

5. Avoid becoming too demanding of your partner or friends' time and attention.

People accustomed to solitude may naturally desire more personal space than others. However, it's crucial to strike a balance in relationships and avoid excessive isolation, as it can create feelings of inequality and distance for your partner or friend.

You will gain the knowledge necessary to interact with others equally when involved and included in your community. You'll gradually learn to support and care for your family, significant others, or friends. With this knowledge, you'll be able to live a fulfilling life and healthily meet your responsibilities. Your future relationships will be free of the stress that has plagued you in your past relationships, allowing you to grow up happy, healthy, and successful. It will take time and consistent practice to learn how to manage your ADHD superpower.

PART II

FROM CHAOS TO CLARITY

5

LEVELING UP: THE EXECUTIVE FUNCTIONS

Developing specific skills can be a game-changer in your life, enabling you to excel in your academic endeavors and career path. Executing these skills can help you achieve your goals, take on leadership roles, and contribute positively to society. Executive function is sometimes called the "brain's management system." These skills empower us to set goals, strategize, and effectively accomplish tasks. When people's executive function is impaired, it affects them at home, school, and their daily lives. Impairments in these areas can cause poor time management and self-control, leading to difficulties in school and work.

EXECUTIVE FUNCTION CATEGORIES:

1. Working Memory

This is the ability to remember information and then put it to use. For example, say you are about to go on a road trip. You need to pack for the trip based on what you already know about your destination. To do this, you should check off your list when you pack items in your suitcase. This is working memory, which helps you remember what you need and is on your to-do list. Working memory also allows us to focus on one thing while ignoring distractions.

2. Cognitive Flexibility (also called flexible thinking)

Cognitive flexibility is your ability to think about things from different perspectives. It means you can look at a problem from many angles and see the big picture. The big picture includes how the issue relates to other problems, how it fits into the overall scheme of things, and how each step leads to the next. Cognitive flexibility is also called creative thinking or "lateral thinking."

3. Inhibitory Control (which includes self-control)

Inhibitory control is the skill that helps us control our impulses and behavior when it's appropriate. It's the ability to delay gratification, manage emotions, resist temptations, and organize ourselves. To have a healthy level of inhibitory control requires understanding the feelings and thoughts that help push our behavior into balance.

ADHD can affect executive functions in many ways. ADHD symptoms such as impulsivity and distractibility interfere with executive functions and can cause difficulties in planning, organizing, and using working memory. It can also make cognitive flexibility challenging to access and hard to maintain a state of self-control.

ADHD AND THE CHALLENGES OF POOR EXECUTIVE FUNCTION

1. Staying on Top of Homework

Many people get started on a task and then find it difficult to continue. Or they may lose track of things as they go along. Poor working memory or poor planning can significantly contribute to these difficulties. For instance, if you struggle with working memory and creating a plan, you might encounter challenges when writing a difficult paper. It can be challenging to organize your thoughts effectively, resulting in a lack of structure. Additionally, suppose you lack a clear starting point or fail to allocate sufficient time for completing tasks before their deadlines. In that case, you may struggle with short-term obligations while neglecting other important tasks.

2. Troubleshooting in Unexpected Situations

Getting stuck on one thing or having difficulty antici-pating events are two ways that you may experience executive function deficits. Flexible thinking and emotional control are required to see the big picture of everyday situations. This requires anticipating prob-lems, thinking strategically, and having a good action plan. For example, if you can't imagine the conse-quences of your actions, you might not think about how your behavior will affect others. Or, if you over-look the real solution to a problem, you may jump from one idea to another, never resolving anything. If you struggle with regulating your emotions and impulses, you may react similarly to an angry outburst and a rude remark.

3. Creating Structure and Schedules

Schedules, deadlines, and organization are demanding for you. It's difficult to "get organized" and maintain being on task.

It's very common to develop routines and particular ways of doing things that are challenging to change. This works well for you in most circumstances. But the routines become difficult to follow when something changes, as in life. You might also get frustrated remembering where vital information is located after spending thirty minutes looking for it and feeling lost. If you set yourself up with clear rules and a plan ahead of time, your task may be easier to complete on time.

4. Shopping and Living on a Budget

Planning, prioritizing, and impulse control are skills required to manage and budget your money, keep track of purchases, and make sound financial decisions. If these skills are impaired, you may not use good judgment when making purchases or doing things that spur rapid spending, or you may buy more than you can afford.

5. Starting a New Project or Activity

You may need help to initiate a project or a goal. This could be because you are easily distracted by something that interests you. Or you might need to figure out where to start or whether your plan will work out how you thought it would. You may be stuck on the first step of a new project because your working memory has been paused, and you can't remember instructions or what to do next. You may also have so many ideas due to your creativity, yet you struggle to organize them from start to finish. As a result, you often spend a lot of time planning and thinking about the task but don't make much progress in completing it.

WHY DOES THIS HAPPEN?

Several things often happen simultaneously when a person has trouble completing a task. Memories are being retrieved (working memory), thoughts are being organized (mental processing), and actions are being planned (executive functions). It's common for elements of each area to be impaired, with some parts intact while others are absent or weak. Suppose some executive functions are affected, but others are relatively intact. In that case, a gap likely exists between the tasks or behaviors you can achieve and those you can do easily.

Having ADHD means that your ability to plan, organize, and manage your behavior is impaired. Suppose you struggle with completing work or staying focused on tasks. In that case, you may experience a gap between your actual achievements and your perceived expectations of what you should be able to accomplish. This gap may be caused by executive function skills that affect how you manage and complete the task.

How executive functions are experienced depends on which processes are impaired and which are not. For example, you may organize your thoughts while ruminating (repetitive, intrusive, mind-wandering) or distract yourself by hyper-focusing on a single task. Both can help you complete tasks but at the expense of focusing on the process of completing the task. Or, you can manage your thoughts during working memory and still have difficulty organizing them into a plan. This would be likely in timed tasks where you're having difficulty keeping up with the demands of your environment as it changes and evolves.

What makes executive function deficits unique is that they are not just technical problems related to attention, motivation, and working memory. As they affect many different areas of life (like social skills, planning, organization, decision-making, and impulse control), the created difficulties are often experienced differently.

ADOLESCENT BRAIN DEVELOPMENT: EXECUTIVE FUNCTION IN TEENS

The adolescent brain is neurobiologically primed for impulsivity and thrill-seeking. This bravado is the result of two separate but interconnected processes. To begin with, myelination, the final stage of neurodevelopment, has yet to be completed. By adolescence, neurons (or brain cells) have migrated correctly, formed connections with neighbors across long distances, selected functional connections, and pruned excess connections. The final step is to insulate the well-functioning neurons to speed up their processing and to myelinate the links, prioritizing speed over the ability to modify associations further. On the other hand, our brains myelinate in stages, completing the brainstem before birth, but only the visual areas once those neurons prune them.

Many myelinates are still in the growth phase, and much of the cortical white matter is incompletely myelinated. Fibers remain uninsulated, allowing some signals to pass through them faster. But this process becomes more efficient with age. Overall, teenagers' brains are more easily distracted by emotionally arousing events and are worse at future planning than adults; this is because the frontal lobes, the center for executive function, where planning, sequencing activities, and prioritizing long-range goals take place, are not fully developed in adolescents. This can lead to impulsivity and risk-taking behavior.

The second factor is that the brain's reward center, the nucleus accumbent, is more active in adolescents and rewards risk-taking and novelty-seeking behavior with pleasure. Scientists have discovered that the prefrontal cortex, which inhibits impulsive behavior, fully develops around age twenty-five (Arain et al., 2012). In other words, adolescents have great difficulty balancing long-range goals with current rewards—especially when they seem to conflict with immediate desires. These findings make it clear that the teenage brain is still developing, and the increased popularity of risky behavior among this age group is not due to a conscious choice by teens. Some teenagers engage in risky behavior because they cannot calculate their actions' potential rewards and consequences. Overall, though you do understand these risks, you may not be able to resist them.

Peer Pressure's Effect on the Adolescent Brain

Peer pressure is a phenomenon to which many people with ADHD are more susceptible. Adolescents may be swayed into certain behaviors they wouldn't usually choose because of peer pressure or other social dynamics and not wanting to feel different. Often, these pressures are amplified due to ADHD and not being well-liked by your peers; that being the case, you may feel an added level of social pressure to conform to gain approval.

You are predisposed to engage in risky behavior and will be even more vulnerable to peer pressure. Engaging in risky behaviors can lead to a release of dopamine in the brain, which creates a sense of pleasure. However, it is crucial to acknowledge that such actions may have consequences that you may not fully recognize. This cycle of seeking pleasure and unawareness of the potential negative outcomes can become addictive.

Peer pressure is not always bad. Some adults get through their teenage years by making good choices and learning from their peers as they go along. We have an inherent ability to learn from our peers because it is ingrained in our nature. This learning period is designed to teach you how to be the good independent versions of yourself who prioritize health and safety over impulsive behavior.

Importance of Executive Functions in School

You may struggle in school and life because certain behaviors impede your executive function, which needs to be addressed to succeed. Executive functions are the highest order thinking processes, contributing to developing all other cognitive functions. Your education, social interactions, and daily life experiences all contribute to developing your executive functions, particularly within the school environment. You may struggle when it comes to paying attention, completing academic assignments, or even day-to-day tasks on time due to difficulty using your executive functions. In addition, you are likely to make careless mistakes, leading to poor grades due to a lack of focus, organization, and planning. The executive function is responsible for planning, self-monitoring, controlling impulses, dealing with complex tasks, and processing information. These abilities significantly contribute to success in school and everyday life situations.

To overcome this obstacle, learning and developing your executive function skills is important. So, how can you improve and strengthen your executive function skills to overcome this obstacle?

6

RETRAINING FOCUS AND PLANNING

P lanning and staying focused to execute your plan are talents that can be learned and are essential for success in school and life. These basic building blocks help you develop and improve your executive function skills.

BOOSTING FOCUS

In a world filled with distractions, we struggle to focus on what matters. Having ADHD doesn't mean you are constantly distracted, but you have a more challenging time staying focused. It also means your focus wanders away from what matters and where it should be. Having ADHD also means your situational or overall attentional awareness is not as sharp as those without it. You may have utilized different techniques for controlling it, but they don't always work. The truth is that focus is more on your brain's function rather than something you do. Your brain can be trained to focus on a single task and filter out distractions effortlessly without requiring excessive effort.

Attentional Control

Attentional control is an executive function ability that entails focusing on specific environmental stimuli while tuning out or ignoring other stimuli.

Attentional control involves two distinct behaviors:

1. Paying attention to a stimulus in the environment

This can be auditory (to words and sounds) or visual (to shapes and colors), or kinesthetic (to touch or movement). Attentional control allows you to maintain focus on a specific stimulus in the environment. For example, you turn down the TV in your room to stay focused when you study. You can be distracted by other stimuli and still pay attention to what matters. If your mind wanders, you need to pay attention. Thus, paying attention is not a choice. It's a necessity.

2. Ignoring or non-attending to others

This is the ability to ignore or non-attend to environmental stimuli even when it is in plain sight. Imagine you are at a party listening to a friend talk. You may notice people at other tables nearby discussing louder than usual, but you will ignore them if this does not interfere with your conversation. Alternatively, if you find yourself in a situation where the conversation with your friend becomes dull at a party, you may naturally gravitate towards someone more engaging or captivating. Attentional control involves tuning out a particular stimulus in the environment, ignoring it, or non-attending to it. Attentional control helps us focus on specific target stimuli in the background and tune out or ignore distractions and irrelevant thoughts.

Focus and concentration loss are the most significant primary setbacks of ADHD. However, you can build them by using the following tips and tricks:

Long-term Srategies

1. Take frequent breaks.

Paying attention during a task is challenging since you are attempting to work on multiple things concurrently. Taking a break from intense concentration may seem contradictory, but it can help you pay attention better. Taking frequent short breaks allows you to be more focused on the job. Breaks should be brief–no more than three to five minutes–but sufficient to restore attentional control and re-establish your focus.

2. Plan physical activity during breaks.

Along with frequent breaks, it's beneficial to incorporate physical activity into those "brain breaks." For example, stand up and walk around if you are sitting at a desk. Or, if you are doing homework, take a few laps around the room. If you have an outlet like a radio or news channel, use it to listen to something fed to the brain that keeps your attention focused. In addition to giving your brain a good workout, physical activity can help you refocus your attention by relaxing the mind and muscles.

3. Break large tasks into smaller parts.

Breaking down long-term tasks into smaller, more manageable parts can be beneficial for tasks that require sustained concentration. This is especially effective for labor-intensive and mentally demanding occupations. Instead of accomplishing the entire goal, focus on one small step at a time. You might achieve a lot of steps in a few minutes and then let your brain rest for a bit before continuing.

4. Test out times for peak attention.

Different people work at different times to get their best work done. It can help to test out times during the day when your attention level is at its peak. You may find that you're at your peak right after you wake up, before an important meeting, after a workout, or between classes. This can help you set a schedule to get the most out of your day.

5. Practice focus in a designated location.

Since distractions can hijack our attention, it can be helpful to practice focusing on the same place at the same time every day, especially if it is a place that is relatively distraction-free. Turn off your phone and other electronics in your designated location and put up posters that stimulate the senses and promote focus. Make sure to use the methods to help stabilize your attention. You can also ensure the space is comfortable, allowing you to take effortless breaks whenever necessary.

6. Use visual timers.

A common way to practice paying attention is by using a timer. This can be something physical, like a clock you must look at to keep track of time or a digital countdown timer like the ones on your computer. This focuses your mind on something that you need to do so that it doesn't wander off, and it also reminds you when it is time to stop being distracted and get back to work.

Practicing these strategies regularly will enhance your attention skills, making staying focused on a single task easier without getting distracted by other thoughts or activities.

Useful Tips and Techniques

Here are some additional tips you can implement to enhance your focus and concentration:

1. Close the door.

This is particularly beneficial in environments with high levels of noise or distractions. Keeping the door closed will help prevent distractions and allow you to focus better.

2. Find your frog and take a tiny bite off of it.

Your most feared chore is known as your "frog." Our minds tend to avoid doing things we don't want to do. We have trouble focusing when something drags us down, so our minds wander to anything else but the task. Concentrating on your frog briefly each day can be helpful, just enough for you to take that first bite and accomplish your task.

3. Use a fun Pomodoro timer.

Pomodoro is named after a tomato-shaped kitchen timer. The Pomodoro Technique is a time management method that aids in focusing on one task at a time. Additionally, it facilitates breaking down large tasks into smaller, manageable steps. This timer has many variations, primarily web-based or mobile app timers. Choose the best option that complements your working style (Wikipedia, Pomodoro Technique).

The Pomodoro Technique process consists of six steps (Better time management for teens, n.d.):

- **Step 1: Choose a task you'd like to get done.** It doesn't matter if it's something big, something small, or something you've been putting off for a million years. What matters is that it merits your complete and undivided attention.
- **Step 2: Set the Pomodoro timer to twenty-five minutes.**
- **Step 3: Continue working on the task until the timer goes off.** Work on your chosen task for twenty-five minutes, focusing only on that task. Don't check your phone or email, and don't answer the doorbell—the only thing you should do is work on that one task!

- **Step 4: Put an "✔" on the paper after the timer rings.**
- **Step 5: Take a small break.** Breathe, stretch, get a glass of water, and do one push-up for fun— whatever you need to do to relax for a moment.
- **Step 6: After four Pomodoros, take a longer break.** Once four Pomodoros have been completed, you can take a longer break. Twenty minutes is adequate. Or thirty. Before the next round of Pomodoros, your brain will use this time to process new information and relax. Try to focus on a single task at any given time. After completing the Pomodoro, repeat this procedure.

4. Mix up your tasks.

Instead of working on one thing for hours and hours, try switching between a few different things every so often. For example, you could do research one day, write a draft another day, and edit it the next day. Or, you could focus on different areas of one project at various times during the week. This will assist in maintaining your focus, prevent becoming bored, and keeping your mind engaged while working on the tasks at hand.

5. Anticipate future obstacles.

Sometimes you get distracted because you don't know how to handle something unexpected. It is a good plan to anticipate potential challenges and proactively devise strategies to overcome them. Try writing out every potential roadblock you'll face while completing a task, and then brainstorm how you'll avoid slipping into that trap. For instance, if you have a speech to deliver, you can anticipate challenges like nerves and stage fright. You can then develop solutions, like practicing your speech in front of a mirror or seeking someone's feedback on your speech and asking them to listen and provide input can be helpful. This plan will help you avoid distractions when it's time for the big event.

6. Look for the jet stream.

Momentum, which allows us to gain confidence and provides assurance that we can complete a task, is the most critical factor. So, look for the flow of energy in your life: is it a good stream of energy or a bad one? If you have a strong energy flow, be happy about it and use that flow to help you maintain focus. If there is no stream of energy in your life, try identifying what you need to build momentum. This could be forming a new habit, starting a new project, or organizing your desk better. Once you have momentum, use that energy to help fuel your work for the day.

7. Write down why this task is meaningful to you.

Research shows that writing down why a task is meaningful to you can improve your ability to focus. So, make a list of meaningful things for yourself and look at them every day. Engaging in this practice can enhance your concentration and motivate you to complete the task at hand.

Some questions worth asking:

- What does the completion of this task give me?

This could be something as simple as a sense of relaxation or accomplishment or something more significant, like furthering your education or mastering a new skill. This might be a little personal, but our feelings of accomplishment are often tied to how we think we will feel after completing a task. So, ask yourself (or write in a journal) how you think you will feel once this project ends. If the answer is "good," you can use that feeling to help motivate and push yourself to get it done!

- Why is this task important to me?

Try asking yourself why you're doing this task. Is it for the money? For validation? For a sense of purpose? Understanding your motivation for undertaking this specific task can serve as a driving force to stay focused and maintain your momentum.

- How will this help me get to where I want to be?

Will this task contribute to the achievement of your plan? Do you have any ideas on how to accomplish this task more quickly? Reflecting on your personal goals and evaluating whether this task aligns with your overarching plan can provide clarity and help you stay on track. Additionally, brainstorming strategies to expedite task completion can enhance efficiency and productivity.

- How can I add value to this project?

Consider what value you could bring to this project. There may be project areas that would benefit from your input or abilities, such as being artistic, that you don't utilize in your current function but could be valuable on another project. If so, consider incorporating those skills into your work tasks and projects.

- How many people will benefit from this task?

If possible, assign a monetary value to the task. This can help you understand its importance and prioritize it accordingly. Some tasks can't be quantified, but if you say that this task will help twenty people, it is an excellent idea to prioritize it above others.

Sometimes a task is awful, and we need help deter-mining why. That's okay! If possible, we should always keep our "why" at the forefront of our minds.

8. Try to beat the clock.

When you can't focus, try to beat the clock. Try to get through the task as fast as possible. This can help you focus and complete a project as soon as possible—you don't have to stick around until the task is perfect. Even though it might seem counterintuitive, consider this: if you spend a day moving quickly and finishing tasks, you'll be able to accomplish more in the same amount of time. Then set goals you can meet in specific time frames (e.g., complete all tasks by 2 p.m.).

9. Be kind to yourself.

Sometimes you need to give yourself extra love and understanding and be kind to yourself. If you find yourself determined to complete a task, but it's not going well, stop momentarily. Take a quick break. Tell yourself it's okay to feel overwhelmed by the task at hand. That's normal! You can always return later when you feel more focused and complete this task!

Remember: If you can't focus, it's not because you're lazy or hopeless, so don't be too hard on yourself.

WITH FOCUS COMES PLANNING

Planning is the secret to achieving your objectives and getting everything, you want. Planning simplifies defining your goals, outlining the steps to achieve them, and setting clear deadlines. It offers a clear sense of purpose and direction for the tasks that need to be completed.

The Basics of Planning

Planning is defined by the Behavior Rating Inventory of Executive Function (BRIEF) as a set of skills connected to an individual's ability to recognize and manage future-oriented tasks.

An individual's planning skills can be categorized as follows:

- Generate and keep to a schedule
- Identify goals, tasks, and sub-tasks
- Monitor progress
- Set new goals when achieving previous ones

Planning skills are frequently intertwined with organizational and prioritization abilities. Your organization skills are organizing your thoughts, physical space, and time. This includes choosing services to complete and what you will focus on first. Your prioritization skills help you determine which tasks need to be completed first and how they will be accomplished.

Why are Planning and Organizational Skills Necessary?

They're important because they help you make decisions to get things done. When you plan and think about your goals, you can complete more projects with less difficulty. Planning also enables you to evaluate your past efforts to make adjustments for your goals in the future.

According to studies (Sippl, 2020), executive function skills such as planning and organizing correspond directly with a variety of performance measures, including:

- Excel in school
- Increase time on task
- Reduce absences or suspensions
- Achieve higher grades
- Lose fewer items
- Interact successfully with family, friends, and peers
- Focus on employment and professional success later in life

How Do Planning Deficits Impact Challenging Behavior?

When you don't plan and organize your tasks, you're more likely to feel overwhelmed by a task. Planning assists in placing a task within its appropriate context and enables you to determine the necessary actions and estimated time required to complete it. A structure can help you achieve your goals, however, without self-imposed structure, your actions may align with the absence thereof.

Below are some examples of how planning may lead to your success in tackling a challenging behavior:

- Planning will help you see if you have the necessary tools to complete a task.
- It will help you determine your daily schedule.
- Planning will help you define goals, which creates motivation for achieving these goals. It will also help you monitor progress.
- Planning enables you to recognize potential problem areas and assists in preventing them from happening.

Essential Planning Skills for Everyone

1. Identify an end goal

Begin by encouraging yourself to identify the final objective of small chores. Consider the purpose of putting away your belongings (so the room is clean) or performing daily duties such as washing the car (to help the family). This motivates you to finish the task much faster.

2. Identify the main idea versus minor details

Once you know what you want to achieve, it's time to think about the main ideas related to it. You may have some details, but it's essential to identify which elements are relevant and which are not. Consider the details that need to be completed to achieve your main idea. For example, if you're cleaning your room, you can use a to-do list to track what needs to be accomplished. Your main idea is that this room is clean, but other details surround it. Check off the relevant item for that area and cross out anything irrelevant.

3. Use a checklist

Next, consider keeping a checklist as you begin your chores. Checklists are excellent tools for staying organized and focused on specific tasks. Having a checklist will help you remember the steps of a routine or process, so it's easier to execute it. While filling out your checklist, you will also practice your planning skills by making plans for each item on the list. You can search for a checklist online and find one most suitable for your needs—perhaps one appropriate for helping with different chores. You may even want to use a checklist to refer to as you complete certain chores. It can be helpful to reflect on your accomplishments and evaluate your progress at the end of each day.

4. Plan simple activities

After completing your checklist, you can complete simple tasks that may not require much planning. If you're not used to keeping a routine or are just getting started, completing one chore at a time is an excellent way to help the new habit stick. For example, if you're cleaning your room, you should begin by cleaning a single area. Once this area is clean, move on to another area or task. For instance, once your bathroom is cleaned, it is time to clean your bookshelf. Your checklist should be simple and easy to follow. Only plan some of the detail of every item on your checklist; try using a step-by-step guide as you complete each task.

5. Use visual maps, drawings, and diagrams

One strategy to help enhance executive function is creating visuals, including mind maps, drawings, and diagrams. Mind mapping is a process by which an individual creates a visual representation of their thoughts. Mind maps have been shown to help individuals learn and retain information more efficiently and make connections between various data sets. A mind map is created in ordered groups of linked words. In this way, you can map out the steps and information of a process. You can also use drawings and colored cards to help organize the mind map further.

Visual maps can be helpful when you want to locate a specific item or acquire knowledge on how to create something specific. Drawings and diagrams can create a visual representation of new ideas. You can draw a simple line to represent the steps you would go through to complete a task or draw what you think your idea may look like when finished. It's also essential to include all necessary details, such as measurements and materials.

6. Use the 'Next Best Step' strategy

If you're trying to complete a large project, you can use this strategy to help break it down into smaller, more manageable steps. This technique also enables you to recognize your progress and feel more motivated to continue what you've started. Next Best Step is a helpful strategy for someone overwhelmed by the size of their project.

The "Next Best Step" strategy is broken down into the following steps:

1. Define your goal
2. Break it down into steps
3. Start with the first step
4. Reward yourself once you've completed a part of the project
5. Repeat as necessary until you have finished the entire project
6. Take action and complete each of the steps
7. Stay motivated by celebrating small successes along the way

7. Communicate a plan

A plan is a written record of who will do what and when. It also sets expectations for everyone who is involved in the process. A good plan is practical; it details how the action will be completed and when it will be accomplished. Plans contain future schedules that allow people to anticipate what they need to do to meet their commitments. When communicating with family, friends, or others, it's essential to be concise and clear when describing your plans. This can include your goals, the steps you have taken so far to reach these goals, and the task you are currently engaged in.

8. Manage things when they don't go according to plan

Managing things will help you continue a task and not let minor setbacks deter you or create additional stress. Don't let it mess with your expectations when you do something different from what you had initially planned. You can stay calm and control the situation by managing things when they don't go according to plan. It also helps maintain a sense of perspective and reminds you that reaching your goals is still possible. Remember to celebrate when you've finished the mission!

No one strategy works perfectly for everyone. However, the techniques mentioned above are helpful for different people based on their needs and struggles. Anyone can use these strategies at any age; this means that all these strategies can be used at any time or place.

7

TIME MANAGEMENT AND ORGANIZATION

Time is the great equalizer among all the resources at your disposal. Every day, we are given the same amount of time, and no amount of riches or skill can buy us more. However, managing and using your time well can significantly impact your productivity and satisfaction. It would help if you devoted substantial time and effort to learning how to manage your time properly and efficiently. You will need adequate time management and organizational skills to excel in academics, work, and everyday life. Setting aside time for studying, keeping up with deadlines, and organizing your work can all help you improve your chances of success. Preparing thoroughly, focusing on one thing at a time, and maintaining a healthy balance of study habits can positively impact your education and success.

THE BASICS OF TIME MANAGEMENT SKILLS

Time management is your ability to estimate, allot, and stay within time constraints and deadlines. According to prominent executive function researchers Dr. Peg Dawson and Dr. Richard Guare, time management abilities are concerned with how we use our time effectively and how that usage affects us and others. Children and young people generally have high time-management skills and can estimate how long chores will take, budget time, and accomplish routines efficiently. Time management is essential for academic achievement, ensuring that all schoolwork, extracurricular activities, and other commitments are completed on time (Sippl, 2020).

Examples of Time Management Skills

Some examples of time management, like other executive function skills that grow and alter throughout a child's development, include:

- Set priorities
- Estimate timelines and budgets
- Plan ahead

- Complete assignments promptly
- Fulfill other responsibilities within the allotted time
- Overcome distractions
- Establish practical, timesaving skills

Why Are Time Management Skills Important?

Time management skills are essential both in your personal life and professional life. Time management will help you accomplish your goals and meet your obligations. This includes everything from completing a book report to attending soccer practice on time. Time management abilities will enable you to make the most of each day, a talent that will be useful in the future. Researchers have examined the relationship between time management and other executive function skills and academic, vocational, and social success. People with ADHD often face challenges with understanding and managing time effectively. So, developing time management skills and learning to utilize this valuable tool to get more out of life is essential.

Someone with well-developed time management skills will:

- Have higher academic achievement.
- Experience the improved economic benefits of stable employment.
- Enhance your quality of life and have better relationships with others (VanDuzer, 2020).

Techniques to Master Time Management

1. Map out the weeks

SMART goals, which are **S**pecific, **M**easurable, **A**ctionable, **R**ealistic, and **T**ime-based, are based on this concept. Every Sunday, set aside some time to sit down and list everything you need to get done for the upcoming week.

Compile a list of items and sort them based on your priorities into the following categories:

- Must be completed (These are frequently referred to as "bottlenecks"—tasks must be completed immediately.)
- I would like to finish (Things that can wait a bit longer.)
- Things to do (Such as recreational activities, hanging out with friends, or watching TV.)

Then write out Monday through Friday, noting how many hours you have for each. Every day should have a start and finish time. Place the various tasks in order of priority and time needed.

2. Use Calendar Updates

Your phone or computer can be beneficial for this time management technique. You can use it to add reminders or notifications to your calendar to ensure you plan your day without overlapping activities or forgetting major tasks or appointments. Create a separate calendar specifically for the things you need to do. Establish check-off boxes that allow items unrelated to those activities (like household chores) to be accounted for. You can also begin recording important dates, like birthdays and days off. Your device notification will remind you when an activity is due. Make a habit of updating your calendar at least once a day. Keep it organized by creating a column of "To Do" items and another column of "Will Do" things.

Add To-Do: These are things you need to get done (but they can wait).

Add Will Do: Will do is for immediate priorities you will accomplish very shortly. Write down a time when you will cross each thing off your list.

This helps you organize tasks, set short-term and longer-term goals, and prevent overlapping activities. Updating your calendar daily makes you less likely to forget necessary appointments and deadlines, and you can plan the people and resources needed to complete each task. You should also add any ideas you have throughout the day.

3. Prep for School the Night BEFORE

This will help with time management because it is always good to prepare for school. Even though it may feel like an extra step, investing time in preparing the night before can significantly benefit you. It allows you to save time and conserve energy for the following day.

Prepare the following the night before:

- Have your binders, books, pencils, pens, or any other materials you need organized and ready, so you don't have to waste time gathering everything together the following day.
- Break down the day into segments of time. Decide what you have to accomplish in the morning and what you'll be able to get done after school.
- Determine your time before school starts and list your priorities for the morning based on that.

- By estimating the required time for each task, you can track your daily progress, helping you stay organized and effectively manage your time.

Reorganize your priorities throughout the day, if necessary, based on things that come up or other unexpected events.

4. Have a Place for Everything

Organizing things is vital to keeping your life organized. Think of ways to keep your desk, cabinets, and home neat.

- Avoid clutter. Avoid having many things lying around (e.g., unnecessary school files) or clutter. Clutter will make finding essential things when you need them more complex, lowering your work productivity.
- Keep important things close for quick retrieval: memos with important dates and appointments, homework assignments, and books with homework (if available).
- If you have a desk at home, allocate one side to holding your supplies, including scissors, pens, markers, and paper clips. Additionally, you can store your books in a cabinet.

- Make sure that there are pens, pencils, paper, and other supplies available for you to use at school.
- If you have a locker, keep all your supplies nearby so you won't have to get everything from your locker each time you use it.

This will help with time management because getting things done when needed will be easier. Disorganization makes it more difficult to find items when you need them.

5. Time Yourself

Time yourself as you complete a task. Knowing exactly how long something takes can also help with time management.

Once you understand the duration needed for specific tasks, you can estimate the time required for other projects more precisely. This helps in planning and managing your time effectively. Do this regularly. Remember that EVERYTHING has an estimated time in which it should be done. Even driving from your house to school has an estimated drive time depending on where exactly your location is compared to school and traffic. Make a list of something that takes a long time to complete and time yourself doing it. This will help later when you have similar tasks to do.

You can also set challenges for yourself by attempting to complete the same task in less time. This can help improve your efficiency and productivity and make specific tasks more entertaining, improve your focus since you are paying close attention to achieving that task faster than usual, and helps you be more creative and find ways to do things more quickly.

6. Use a Planner

Planning things out in advance can help you manage your time and reduce your anxiety and stress. A planner lets you write your tasks, ongoing assignments, and meetings. Finding items when you need them becomes effortless when you keep all your belongings in a designated place. This organization method saves you time and frustration, as you no longer have to search various locations. It avoids double booking a specific time slot.

A planner can also benefit schoolwork and studying because you know when your assignments need to be delivered or studied for and when exams are, making everything much more organized. You require less time finding and writing things down, the information you need is always in one place, and keeping everything filed away is easy. You can also use a planner for all your homework projects.

How to work on a planner:

- List all your upcoming assignments (work-related and other school work) alphabetically to find everything easily.
- Write due dates for assignments. If you're in college and have papers due every week, make sure they're listed near the top, so you'll remember to start working on them as soon as they arrive.
- Keep a separate section for your daily tasks and other to-do lists that are constantly being updated. Deleting items is extremely difficult if you're trying to track everything.
- Check off completed tasks and note complete periods (or days).
- Set up a rota system with friends so that responsibilities can be divided up. This will help with time management. There are fewer distractions when everyone has things they need to get done because everyone's roles are clear.
- Use color codes for specific activities, for example, green for doctor appointments, red for sports activities, yellow for rest time, etc.

7. Budget and Prioritize Sufficient Time to Complete a Task

Plan the time you have left to complete a task and see if you have enough time. Be realistic, allocating specific time to each activity. If you realize you don't have sufficient time to complete a task, it is suggested to avoid attempting it altogether. Prioritizing tasks based on the available time and resources is crucial, ensuring efficient and effective completion.

Making deliberate choices about how you allocate your time is pivotal. It empowers you to prioritize activities that align with your goals, values, and responsibilities. By being aware and conscious of how you spend your time, you can maximize productivity, achieve better work-life balance, and pursue activities that bring fulfillment and satisfaction. If you do not use that time, you waste that time slot. Make sure you prioritize tasks based on their importance and how much time you use for each task. This will give you a clear understanding of the remaining time in the day, ensuring that tasks are completed on time.

8. Increase Work Speed to Complete a Deadline but Avoid Rushing Around Except on Rare Occasions

Deadlines are specific times by which you have to finish something. For example, an assignment is due at 10:00

138 | LEILA MOLAIE

a.m. on Friday. You need to finish it in time to ensure you meet your deadline. In this case, you will either get a lower grade or miss the chance to submit the assignment. Deadlines are critical to helping keep things in order and to structure your success. Use a planning technique called 'deadline setting" to complete tasks so they will be done on time.

To plan how long a task will take, use a timer or stopwatch, and set deadlines for each step of the work process using this method:

- Create different categories for different tasks (e.g., "3 hours of study, 3 hours of writing, two days of editing, one month of circulation" or "1 day of reading and a half-hour of review").
- Set deadlines for each category a week in advance.
- Develop a detailed plan for each step (e.g., what you will do during the work period) and the time it will realistically take to complete each step.
- After creating the plan and setting deadlines for each task, set the actual dates for working on that task.
- When you begin each task, record the date and time. Start with the highest priority task and progress downward.

- When you are finished with a task, check it off. If you don't finish it on a set day but would like to finish earlier, move the deadline ahead and give yourself more time to work on it. For example, if you need three hours of studying for an exam that is worth 30 percent of your grade and only fifty minutes are left on Tuesday night, don't do something else (like watch TV or chat online) until you get it done because it will take longer than fifty minutes. Then, you'll have to spend even more time doing it later.

Everyone has unique preferences and needs when it comes to organization. **Having a routine and being disciplined is the key.** Exploring different methods and finding what works best for you is important. Don't let others' opinions discourage you. The critical approach is to try different strategies and discover the ones that best suit you in the long run.

Before You Begin (Task Initiation)

The capacity to start a task on your initiative is known as task initiation. It can cover a range of abilities, such as coming up with ideas on your own, resolving issues, and following directions without assistance. Task initiation is one of the core executive function skills, along with time management and planning, and it can pose specific challenges, especially for individuals with ADHD.

Task initiation and time management skills are related, as they are intertwined.

Examples of Task Initiation Skills

- Identify an appropriate task, determine a plan of action, and initiate the action.
- Develop strategies that will help you achieve a goal.
- Respond to instructions and follow directions.
- Participate in group activities, such as chatting with classmates or coordinating playtimes.
- Initiate and participate in play, school projects, and homework.

Why Are Task Initiation Skills Important?

Task initiation skills are essential in all aspects of your personal and professional life, whether at home, school, or work. Task initiation is related to time management, and the two can easily be confused. However, task initiation is more closely associated with the ability to start a task without rehearsal or help from others. Once you've grasped some of the advantages of task initiation, you will understand that improving your self-initiative is a great way to get more out of yourself.

ADHD DECODED | 141

People with well-developed self-initiative:

- Are independent and able to work without much supervision.
- Have better academic performance.
- Are more positive and patient.
- Experience more success academically and personally.

How to Develope the Task Initiation Skill?

1. Add More Energy

Can you use your energy to initiate something? Or is your energy out of control without you exerting any control over it? Saying "yes" and "no" is the best approach to direct your energies. You'll have more energy if you concentrate on the most crucial tasks. The key is to think about how important the task you want to do is. Then, think about why it's important. The most important tasks with a closer deadline should be the priorities, and the less important tasks with a different deadline can be delayed, as they don't need as much attention right away. If it's unimportant, ask yourself if it needs to be done. If it does need to be done, decide whether the timing is appropriate and whether you're ready for this task. Make sure you want to do the task before starting it. If the answer is "no" or "not yet," wait until you are energized before taking on a new task or project.

2. Break the Major Projects into Smaller Tasks

If you're having trouble with self-initiation because a task is too much or if you're overwhelmed by the amount of structure, a project, or the demands of your schedule, try breaking it into smaller and more manageable steps. This approach makes it easier to stay focused and motivated as you complete each smaller task, ultimately leading to the successful completion of the more significant task. This will help decrease over-whelm and associated anxiety. Then, identify the step you have the most difficulty with (usually initiation). After identifying this step, work on completing just that step before taking on other parts of the task.

You can use hierarchical structures to organize your large task. Try breaking your tasks into smaller steps. The crucial point is to discover a system that suits you best.

- Use a calendar or planner to plan when and where to work on specific tasks.
- Set up weekly, monthly, or long-range goals. If these goals are too big, break them down into smaller steps and identify the first step in

accomplishing the goal or project. These smaller steps help you stay on track toward achieving your goal or completing a project or task.

- Utilize a folder or notebook to keep the smaller steps orderly. Keeping track of smaller steps will help you stay on track toward accomplishing your goal or project or completing a task.
- You can create an outline for the projects or major plans.

3. Get Help

If you have trouble getting an idea or inspiration, ask someone (a parent, teacher, or peer) for help to give you ideas on what project you should do next, or try to find an alternate way or a shortcut that could be used to complete a specified task in less time to get the needed outcome. Ask people for help, especially when you become stuck or need an alternative point of view. If possible, look up information online or talk with peers and older students who have already completed similar tasks. People who have already completed similar projects can offer valuable insight on changing your approach or completing the project more effectively.

These strategies for task initiation can help you get the ball rolling. You can improve your proficiency in these strategies and eventually implement them effortlessly with practice. You will improve self-initiation and increase your performance in school, a job, or a work environment.

8

MENTAL SKILLS TO ENHANCE YOUR ABILITIES

Your most powerful tool, your mind, can be utilized for both positive and negative purposes. Directing your thoughts, actions, and intentions toward constructive or harmful endeavors is within your control. By harnessing the potential of your mind for good, you can create positive change, make meaningful contributions, and cultivate personal growth. Different forces can influence your mind: what others think or say, what you see or read, and how you feel. This can lead to distraction, confusion, and frustration. Your mind needs training and practice to become a positive force in your life. This chapter explores problem-solving, flexibility, and working memory skills which can be useful for your school and work experiences.

GEARING UP FOR SOLUTIONS

Your mind is powerful and allows you to solve problems and make decisions. Problem-solving is vital, as it empowers you to overcome obstacles and effectively handle any crisis. Learning and implementing effective problem-solving techniques can enhance your ability to navigate challenges successfully.

What Is Problem-Solving?

According to Rastogi et al. (2018), "A problem is a situation in which we cannot reach our goals due to some problem or situation.". We engage in problem-solving activities when we examine possible subsequent actions and then take action to achieve a goal.

Some executive function behaviors are involved in problem-solving, including:

- Attention Control
- Planning
- Starting the task

You must consider your surroundings to notice a problem, describe different tactics, and test one. Depending on the circumstances, there might be instances when you need to utilize your organizational, emotional, or time management skills. Working memory and self-monitoring behaviors may influence your problem-solving skills if you observe your behavior and understanding of the environment.

Example of Problem-Solving

Depending on the situation, you may address problems differently. Here are some of the skills you'll need to tackle problems effectively:

- Analyzing and identifying what you need to do,
- Knowing when you have achieved your goal,
- Setting realistic goals for yourself,
- Reacting calmly to unexpected problems,
- Thinking creatively about alternative actions or ideas that may help with the problem.

Problems are often viewed as negative because they are hurdles to success. Anything we don't know can indeed be considered a problem. Even if you know the solution, it may take time to find it. If you cannot solve a problem, it may cause stress, depression, and anxiety. However, there are times when problems sharpen our minds and increase our knowledge or skills.

Developing Problem-Solving Behaviors

As infants and toddlers, our play habits aided in developing problem-solving skills. Much of our "child's play" during this development period consists of cause-and-effect activities or "figuring out how things operate." Problem-solving encompasses decision-making and turn-taking as we progress through our early learning years. We learn to develop creative solutions to easy problems and recognize difficulties when others do. As we age, we start seeing problems in various contexts, including our home, school, employment, and friends, and we try to resolve conflicts and make decisions. In the meantime, we may seek adult advice and support to weigh the potential benefits and drawbacks. Adult problem-solving skills entail finding unique answers to complex challenges and sticking with several solutions until the problem is solved.

The IDEAL Problem-Solving Method

Bransford and Stein (1984) produced one of the most widely used and respected problem-solving approaches actively utilized in industry and education to assist students in identifying an issue, coming up with solutions, and moving forward swiftly and efficiently to this date. Using each stage of the IDEAL model, you can learn steps to confidently approach a challenge.

The IDEAL Problem-Solving Method includes:

I - Identify the Problem

It's impossible to create a solution to an issue without first understanding its extent. Describe the problem in your own words. Outline the known and unknown information about the problem. Exploring all the facts about a situation will help you understand its scope.

Example:

There are several ways to describe the problem. You can label the issue as a "homework challenge" or a "homework-related problem." Then you can pinpoint the exact problem, such as "I'm having difficulty doing my homework on time." It would help if you had gained a clearer understanding of the topic at hand by now. You can name something else that might be problematic, such as "I want to get all my homework done before turning it in." That problem is called a "concern" and helps you focus on your main goal.

D - Define an Outcome

You need to know the desired outcome. Your goals will guide your decisions and actions. By making informed choices and taking decisive action, you will develop a keen sense of foresight and a clear understanding of what to expect at every stage. This clarity enables you to navigate through challenges with greater confidence and adaptability, seize opportunities, and progress toward your goals with purpose and direction. It may be challenging for you to define outcomes and goals.

Example:

"I want to finish all my homework on time to spend time with my family." Here, the outcome is defined as "finish all my homework on time." That is a very real expectation. You may break this down as "finish all homework by 9:00 p.m. daily." As you navigate through the stages of the problem-solving process, considering outcomes and goals will prove beneficial. You'll also know that you're making realistic choices.

E - Explore Possible Strategies

Once you have an outcome, you need to think about the best way to reach it. Using your problem-solving skills, come up with as many strategies as possible that you could use to achieve the outcome. Thoroughly examine each option and the outcome it will produce. Use strategies that make sense and is less complicated.

Example:

The outcomes dictate this step of the process in a variety of ways. First, you can explore accurately what you need to do to achieve your desired outcome.

Strategies may include "work more efficiently," "ask for help," or "do my homework earlier." For the outcome of "finish homework by 9:00 p.m." you may explore the strategy of "work hard for one hour before dinner and then take a break." You can consider the actions you need to take to reach this stage, such as "organize my thoughts on the first page of the assignment sheet."

A – Anticipate Outcomes & Act

You now have a shortlist of possible strategies for reaching your defined outcome. You should evaluate each strategy and look for the outcomes it will produce. If you don't think a strategy will lead to an important outcome, don't use it—start over, you can always try another option.

Example:

You have identified several possible strategies for finishing homework on time. You may do more homework early in the week to have time over the weekend to complete all your assignments. As you proceed through this step, think about how the outcome of each strategy will affect the outcome of your initial problem. If one tactic does not appear to provide a viable answer, you might want to try a new approach. If a strategy does provide valuable input toward success, then put that possible solution through further evaluation as described below.

L – Look and Learn

The last and crucial step in the problem-solving process is to learn from the discoveries made along the way. By reflecting on the effectiveness and limitations of different strategies, one can gain valuable knowledge that directly impacts future decision-making. Understanding what works and what doesn't help determine the next course of action, enabling continuous improvement and adaptation and ensuring ongoing growth and development. This approach allows you to refine your methods and make better decisions in similar situations in the future.

Example:

Doing homework early in the week could solve the problem of completing assignments on time. However, you aren't sure it will work due to prior experiences with several students having similar problems and using various strategies that may have mixed results. Fortunately, you have a friend who has successfully used this strategy. Based on this individual's experience, you decide to try homework early every day so that you can do your assignments on time. This demonstrates the process of observation and learning to find a solution.

BE FLEXIBLE

If living through a pandemic has taught us anything, adjusting to unforeseen change is crucial (and challenging). As your and everyone else's lives were flipped entirely upside down (some more drastically than others), we learned flexibility is the skill you can rely on most when things get challenging and unpredictable.

What Is Flexibility?

Flexibility is commonly understood as the capacity to switch between activities and demands in response to environmental changes. Planning and organizing skills, for example, are considered components of flexibility because they enable a person to shift gears and refocus when new demands and priorities arise.

Five main features characterize every instance of flexibility:

- Adaptability and responsiveness to environmental changes
- Ability to adapt quickly to changing circumstances
- Readiness for change

154 | LEILA MOLAIE

- Capacity for adjusting and managing the transition process
- The ability to adapt and react appropriately to change or unfamiliar circumstances.

The capacity for adapting or adjusting depends in part on one's ability to self-regulate responses, attentional shifts, emotional reactions, and other behaviors that serve a protective function in response to change. Individuals with ADHD often have problems in all these areas.

Developing Flexibility Skills

Early in life, you begin to learn flexibility and build flexible thinking. As a toddler or young child, you would perform basic puzzles and games and engage in play that involved transitioning from one activity to another. As a young child, you learn to move from activity to activity and begin to manage transitions and unexpected shifts without displaying irritable behaviors. Then, as you mature into an adolescent and your social network expands, you are exposed to many scenarios involving challenges and unforeseen happenings. On the other hand, adults are nearby to help and educate you on how to change dynamically.

As you mature into a teenager and young adult, you will be expected to manage unpredictable changes in routines, meet the changing demands of school, employment, and family, and cope with challenging situations. You may occasionally need additional assistance, but you can pivot and recover swiftly when the unexpected occurs if you have well-developed executive function skills.

Why Is Flexibility Necessary?

Flexibility training has several practical advantages.

Successfully managing unexpected changes and acquiring new knowledge has been associated with numerous positive outcomes in individuals of all ages, including:

- Improved reading skills
- Improved resiliency in the face of adversity
- Adults have a greater ability to respond to stress
- Enhanced imagination and problem-solving abilities
- Better working memory and inductive reasoning ability
- Greater overall success in life as you get older

Although flexibility training is universal, you are more prone to having trouble when it comes to shifting between activities, regulating emotions, and managing multiple tasks. Learning or practicing flexibility can help you to overcome some of these difficulties. The most effective way of dealing with the daily challenges of having ADHD is learning to be flexible by developing it as a skill. Naturally, flexibility training becomes even more critical as you develop into an adult and your world becomes increasingly complex (Sippl, 2021).

Cognitive Flexibility Strategies

1. Learn When You Need to Be Flexible

You'll often go through the same routine—from driving to school, eating breakfast, and getting ready for the day until you walk into your first class. The following day, you repeat the process once more. This can be a problem if life throws you a curveball, like a sudden change in your daily schedule or being assigned an in-class presentation on a topic that's not your forte. Consequently, you must know when to be adaptable and what to do when unplanned changes arise. Before bed, you must reflect and ask yourself, "What if?" For example, what if there's an unexpected traffic delay when you're running late to work? Or what if the main entrance is locked, and you need to enter the building quickly? The idea here is to consider the odds and how you'll handle different situations beforehand. This way, you'll know exactly what steps to take when they arise.

2. Plan Ahead

Your impulsive personality makes planning difficult, but it's necessary for organizing your time. You'll be better able to do this after you write out important tasks you need to accomplish. For instance, if football practice is scheduled after school, but you have a doctor's appointment, add this task to your list and write down what you will do before and after the activity. Also, at the end of every day, reflect on how much time you spent doing homework compared to other activities.

Utilizing apps or programs designed for goal setting and task tracking may allow you to be more creative with your planning methods. They can assist you in recalling your tasks and deadlines, serving as reminders when you are tempted to procrastinate.

3. Decide If It's a Change or a Problem

Whenever an unanticipated change affects your actions, deciding whether this is a problem or something that must be altered is essential. For instance, when your teacher emails the class about a change in the morning assignment, it may initially feel like a problem. However, it is crucial to approach it with a positive mindset and reassess the situation. Can you adapt your work style or reconsider the assignment requirements? Keeping a present-focused perspective will help you navigate such situations effectively.

If a problem is presented, you need to ask yourself the following questions:

- What effect will this have on me and the people around me?
- How can I best deal with it at this moment?
- What else can be done to reduce any consequences that may occur as a result?

By thinking through these questions ahead of time, you're more likely to know how best to navigate changes and handle problems in advance.

4. Develop a Routine

Once you have determined that a specific adjustment is necessary, you must create a routine that will work best for you. There are numerous advantages to establishing a routine. First, you can use it as a basis for maintaining flexibility. The more time you invest in enhancing your flexibility, the more likely you will increase your overall cognitive performance. Second, establishing routines increases awareness of when and how your schedule changes.

The key here is developing routines and sticking with them by building flexibility into your everyday life, even when things don't go according to plan. Try not to let the unexpected interfere with routine chores and tasks. Instead, anticipate problems and plan your response. A well-planned routine will significantly improve your ability to deal with unexpected changes.

5. Be Curious

Cultivating a sense of curiosity toward everything in your surroundings is essential. It enhances your flexibility and adaptability when confronted with unexpected changes. Regarding flexibility, you can respond to a change by trying a new approach or thinking about things from multiple angles.

6. Don't Feel Guilty

Nothing is wrong with feeling guilty when you don't act as expected. It's a clear sign that you have high standards and expectations for yourself. This can be empowering as you consistently strive to do what is right and uphold your values in any circumstance or situation. It is important not to let guilt dictate your actions and address the issue promptly when it arises.

7. Be Rational

Before taking any action, consider whether your action is essential or rational. If you evaluate the situation rationally, you might not get upset about what happened. Ultimately, you can accept the results and see that their actions were unnecessary and were undertaken to fulfill some personal need or desire, which is not in their best interest. This will help you to avoid unproductive stress or frustration and unnecessary action.

8. Stay Calm

Cognitive flexibility depends on staying calm. You're not likely to react emotionally or get carried away when relaxed. Inconsistencies occur in everyday life, and these inconsistencies can seriously affect our moods, emotions, and behavior. Cognitive flexibility helps you to be able to deal with change and the unexpected. Remember that flexibility is developed over time through practice and the ability to learn from past experiences.

TOTAL RECALL—WORKING MEMORY

Like a computer, your brain has a finite capacity for storing, retrieving, and recalling information. Working memory is your ability to identify knowledge later when you need it. Working memory is frequently linked to academic subjects such as reading and math. Both capabilities necessitate memorizing knowledge such as letter sounds, sight words, and basic math facts like addition and subtraction. Because you must recall all task components while completing the stages in order, working memory can also include our ability to follow multiple-step directions and complete multi-tasking situations.

Working Memory and Other Executive Function Skills

Working memory is linked to other executive function skills and academic accomplishment. Working memory is more than just short-term memory; it also demands you use it when needed. Working memory is not just information retention; it's also about the application.

As a result, improving working memory can improve other executive functions. Research demonstrates that:

- A solid working memory aids concept creation and integration of old and new information.
- Improvements in working memory can increase attentional control and the ability to stay on task more readily.
- Working memory plays an important role in flexible thinking skills, such as shifting focus

and applying different rules in various situations. This can contribute to improved impulse control and adaptability.

- Working memory is associated with improved performance on other tasks requiring numerical processing, such as arithmetic and math.
- Improvements in working memory are associated with improvements in short-term memory.

Working memory can be used to recall information quickly for non-academic subjects, such as reading comprehension and writing (Sippl, 2021).

Examples of Working Memory Skills

Students should know how to effectively apply working memory skills to solve problems on tests in the classroom. But in real life, working memory includes:

- Ability to effectively multitask
- Ability to remain calm in the face of adversity
- Thinking logically about alternative solutions or how to approach a problem
- Remembering directions on how to get from point A to point B

- Reading and retaining information from a textbook or book chapter
- Keeping in mind the rules for various sports while playing them
- Remembering past lessons about social skills when interacting with others
- Memorizing facts, dates, and names of classmates
- Keeping track of the steps in a project, such as building a bike or something else

Importance of Dynamic Working Memory

Working memory is a cognitive skill that can significantly impact your learning ability and task completion at home, from learning a new language and writing an essay to remembering what to do in an emergency. Working memory relates to placing what you've learned while applying it during a test requiring critical thinking. Working memory should be developed with repetition and practice. This is a trainable skill and strength-based instead of weaknesses-based.

Training Your Brain to Boost Working Memory

1. Train with puzzles

Puzzles have been proven to improve working memory and attention, especially those that use spatial thinking. Sudoku, crossword and word puzzles, jigsaw puzzles, and connect-the-dots improves your spatial skills and help you retrieve information, especially when remembering a series of instructions or keeping track of the steps involved in a project.

2. Try mind-training games

Brain-training apps such as Lumosity and Peak have been increasingly popular in the past decade, developing in lockstep with the growth of smartphones, smartwatches, fitness trackers, and other devices. The primary objective is to enhance information processing speed and expand working memory capacity. The tester offers a variety of questions that you can answer at your own pace and evaluate your performance by scoring yourself once you have finished all the questions. After the test, you can examine the questions you answered incorrectly or failed to answer within the provided time frame.

Memory games are like puzzles because they rely on the practice to remember previous events. This is called episodic memory, one of the key components of working memory. You can also play with friends and family by creating a grid and taking turns placing various objects in designated cells according to specific rules. Some standard games are Concentration and Pairs, which often involve swapping cards around the board so that you can match similar images together.

3. Use analogy to improve your working memory

Analogies are among the few activities that force you to utilize your working memory skills by comparing different words. Analogies are a great way to exercise your frontal lobe, one of the most active areas during working memory.

There are two methods to achieve this:

1. **Write down different facts and then connect them in one coherent sentence.** For instance, you can start by writing down a fact like "Two castles are side by side." Then you can add to the sentence, such as "One castle is big, and the other is small." The key here is to make your sentence one cohesive piece of information you can use later. This will train strong working memory by keeping track of facts in your mind and integrating them into one piece of related learning material

2. **Make a sentence with five different words,
   then write down the sentence as an analogy**.
   For example, write a sentence like, "The plane
   flies high in the air." Then you can make
   an3other analogy that connects four other
   words to this sentence, such as "The plane is
   like a bird because it travels freely through the
   sky." There are various other ways to use
   metaphors in everyday life that do not involve
   repeating a word in the same sentence. For
   example, you could write a sentence that
   connects two words distinct from one another.
   You could compare "a tree" to "a cellphone" or
   "the moon" to "the sky," for example.

4. Play memory games using physical objects

Memory games are a fun way to exercise your working
memory because they can be played in many ways. You
can play the game based on pictures, making up stories
about what is involved in the picture and how many
differences are between each image. You can also create
games that involve objects and rules from scratch.

Any object can be used to play a memory game because
the rules make the game and not the underlying object.
As an example, you can play a game where you have to
remember which person sat in each car seat based on a

specific characteristic assigned to each individual. This game can be more challenging than it initially appears, especially if you attempt to recall all the information simultaneously. As more players join the game, the difficulty level rises as you need to hold and manage a larger amount of information in your working memory.

5. Use your imagination to boost your working memory skills

A great way to use your working memory is by taking the time to visualize the outcome. You often don't need to remember all the details about a subject. Instead, developing a mental image that combines everything into one cohesive whole would be more helpful. This image can be a reference point in future conversations or presentations. Making up stories and mental images is also the basis of episodic memory, which is why they function well with working memory games. For example, they allow you to develop your comprehension skills by placing yourself in different situations and imagining how they will appear. Although this might sound far-fetched, it's a great way to build your imagination and make your working memory more powerful.

6. Memorize information using images and stories

When you take the time to memorize new information, it is stored as memories in the neocortex region of your brain. When you recall that information later, the connections between these memories pull the information back into your active working memory. Therefore, it is helpful to develop a mental image or personal story that can summarize all the facts associated with one piece of information. For example, suppose you are trying to memorize all amendments to a particular bill. In that case, you can create a mental image representing each amendment and how it will affect the document. This is a perfect way to work on your working memory because it allows you to generate more information in your mind at any given time.

Developing working memory is crucial as it enhances your learning abilities and overall performance in various aspects of life. Whether at work, home, or school, practicing and consistently optimizing your working memory skills is essential for excelling in any task.

You can improve your effectiveness in different activities by utilizing your working memory to its full potential. Regular practice is the most effective way to enhance your working memory. With consistent effort, you can make notable improvements. To maintain your working memory skills throughout life, you must continue training regularly throughout your life.

9

SELF-MONITORING AND IMPULSE CONTROL

Self-monitoring is an executive function skill. Many other executive function skills, such as planning, organization, and time management, fall into place when you demonstrate well-developed self-monitoring skills. Your ability to monitor what you do and when and how you should do it is a key factor in your academic performance and social life success.

UNDERSTANDING SELF-MONITORING

Self-monitoring is an executive function skill that involves comprehending your own actions and making necessary adjustments for future improvement. Work-checking behaviors (reviewing mistakes, fixing errors, etc.) and social behaviors are self-monitoring skills

172 | LEILA MOLAIE

(responding to social norms, situational awareness, apologizing, etc.) that help govern your behavior. From home to school, from playing with your friends to completing homework assignments, your ability to self-monitor and control your actions, thoughts, and emotions significantly impacts all aspects of your life.

Self-monitoring is the skill that allows you to adapt and change, helping you become more aware of your actions, emotions, and thoughts to manage them effectively. It is a key executive function skill used in daily life that includes paying attention to details, ensuring your homework gets done on time, and remembering to complete any chores or responsibilities at home or school.

The Benefits of Self-Monitoring to Behaviors for Personal Growth

Like other executive function skills, self-monitoring can be applied to many areas of your life. These skills help you pay attention to details, remember information, and complete tasks that may seem pointless at the time. When self-monitoring skills are disrupted, it creates symptoms such as attention problems and impulsivity. Individuals who engage in self-monitoring at high rates demonstrate the following positive aspects:

- Increased task performance
- Reduced frequency of disruptive behaviors
- Increased efficiency with daily tasks
- Fewer violent and destructive behaviors
- Increased pro-social behaviors, such as initiating interactions, cooperating, and listening

With proactive planning and foresight, you can stay on track with your responsibilities at home and in your studies. After learning a self-monitoring system, you will require less direct supervision from adults and be able to self-regulate. It also helps you plan and make decisions before acting, giving you more control over your direction in life.

ADHD and Self-Awareness

Self-awareness, or metacognition, is an essential executive function skill that aids in monitoring, comprehending, and retaining information. Metacognition is associated with neurobiological structures that regulate memory, concentrated attention, and self-monitoring. It enables you to connect the dots, see the big picture, self-evaluate, monitor, improve performance, and complete tasks. This awareness aids in improving time management, planning, monitoring, and evaluating your approach to a task, your progress, and how close you are (or are not) to achieving your ultimate goal. It applies to social situations and understanding your strengths and weaknesses in yourself and others, which helps you to relate to the people around you.

Consistent practice and dedication can enhance your ability to recognize your thought processes, effectively solve problems, and consciously direct your attention. These skills develop over time with deliberate effort and perseverance.

How Can You Practice Metacognition?

With the right strategies, activities, and ideas, you can learn how to manage your ADHD symptoms and become more self-aware.

Step 1: Identify Your Thoughts and Feelings

This heightened awareness facilitates the development of a plan and enhances your ability to refine your ideas and interactions with others. Consequently, when faced with a situation that elicits emotions like anger or frustration, you can consciously decide how to respond thoughtfully and constructively. There are various approaches you can engage in this process, including:

- Reflect on your emotions by asking yourself how you feel.

- Examine your thoughts to gain insight into what is happening in your mind.
- Visualize alternative perspectives, beliefs, or actions to explore new ways of thinking and behaving. One simple technique is to write or draw a word or phrase on paper, such as "I can control my emotions," to reinforce positive beliefs. This exercise helps you gain perspective by creating positive affirmations.
- Make a list of the specific behaviors that caused your feelings e.g., I get frustrated whenever.....
- List all your feelings, even the ones you avoid, don't want to think about, or make you uncomfortable, e.g., sadness, hatred, and hopelessness.
- Answer the question, "Why do I think that way?"
- Evaluate your thoughts. Ask yourself why you are preoccupied with the thought, e.g., "What is my thought telling me?"
- Ask yourself if you are engaging in faulty thinking.

Skipping this step can lead to various symptoms of ADHD, such as procrastination. Thus, you get so busy with activities that you become unproductive, fail to accomplish anything, and lose sight of what matters most, e.g., watching a TV show to avoid doing your math homework because you struggle with math.

Step 2: Understand Your Thoughts

You can learn to respond to and control these negative, unproductive thoughts if you are aware of your thoughts. This enables you to recognize when these thoughts negatively affect your behavior or performance and provides a way to deal with them without acting on them.

To begin, you can evaluate your thoughts in the following ways:

1. **Ask yourself how you feel.** Is this thought making you feel better? Or is it making you worse?
2. **Ask yourself what is behind your thoughts.** Do they make sense to others? Does your thought need backup information?
3. **Frequently ask yourself, "What if I were thinking about something else right now?"** This will assist you in setting reasonable goals for yourself. You can also ask, "What would I do if I weren't thinking about this right now?"
4. **Label your thoughts.** It helps to break them down and give them some context.

5. **Visualize a new or different way of doing or thinking.** The objective is to develop adaptability in your thinking and effectively manage your responses.

Step 3: Understand Your Behavior

You can train yourself through practice to recognize when and how ADHD symptoms emerge and begin to cope with them. This will help you balance your actions, reducing the frequency of symptoms and acting on them.

As you increase your awareness and understand your abilities and limitations, you can also start asking yourself some questions about your behavior:

1. What am I thinking?
2. What is my intention (goal)?
3. How is this thought affecting my behavior?
4. What is the outcome of this behavior?
5. How can I improve this behavior?

It is important to understand both your strengths and weaknesses to accomplish your goals. You can assess your behavior in different ways:

- Ask your parents or a trusted friend for their opinion about your strengths and weaknesses
- Use one of the self-assessment scales that is geared toward identifying ADHD symptoms, e.g., Conners Adult ADHD Rating Scale, or Barkley Adult ADHD Rating Scale
- When writing about yourself, it's important to highlight your positive traits and provide as much information as possible such as "I am a good leader," "I can stay calm in tense situations," and "I have a lot of friends" and negative traits like "I have trouble paying attention," "I frequently interrupt others while they are speaking," and "I find it challenging to finish tasks I start."

You can learn from your strengths and put them to use to strengthen your weaknesses by:

1. Understanding your strengths
2. Accepting your weaknesses
3. Determining what the effects of your behavior are on others and your environment

4. Understanding how these weaknesses interfere with many aspects of life
5. 5Asking others for feedback (e.g., friends or family) about your strengths and weaknesses
6. 6Develop strategies to improve upon your weaknesses (e.g., learning a new skill, asking for feedback)

Step 4: Apply Your Knowledge

This step involves taking action based on how you think, feel, and evaluate your thoughts. You do it throughout your life to plan for the future and keep working towards goals that matter to you. It also enables you to meet your objectives and live more effectively with ADHD, reducing symptoms.

You can approach these steps in different ways. You don't need to use all of them simultaneously. If you're unsure where to begin, look for signs of feeling stuck, such as overwhelmed, frustrated, or anxious. The main goal is to learn a new way of thinking and manage your thoughts and behaviors to improve the quality of your life. If you notice that your changes are short-lasting and you feel stuck again, reassess your steps and make changes were needed. After each session, take a moment to evaluate regardless of whether they proved beneficial or not to you. Ask yourself, "Did discussing my goals make me feel more in control?" This reflection guides your future progress.

As you develop the skills mentioned earlier, you will enhance your self-awareness and become more adept at thinking before acting or engaging in unnecessary unplanned actions. In conclusion, metacognitive skills can help you manage symptoms and improve interpersonal relationships. It helps you become more self-aware, recognize your strengths and weaknesses, and gain insight into your thoughts and emotions.

A BURST OF IMPULSES

Impulse is doing something without thinking or considering a more reasonable way. Impulses can also be defined as actions or behaviors that you don't plan or are unexpected. Impulsivity is a cognitive tendency that makes it difficult to stop yourself from acting on random or unpredictable thoughts and actions. Many people with ADHD experience impulsive behavior, so learning how to manage impulsivity is essential.

What Is Impulse Control?

It is one of the many executive function skills that enable independent social participation. Impulse control, known as self-control or inhibition, is a set of behaviors that help us "think before acting." When you have impulse control, you can prioritize your wants and needs and resist or avoid doing things that are potentially harmful to yourself or others.

The following are examples of impulse control:

- Taking turns in conversations and permitting others to speak or express their opinions.
- Practicing sharing favorite items, such as treats, snacks, and screen time.
- Having screen time limits.
- Completing difficult or undesirable tasks first.
- Resisting peer pressure to engage in risky or harmful behaviors.
- Avoiding backhanded comments, whining, and negotiations.
- Resisting the urge to vent frustrations during presentations.
- Staying away from risky activities and substances.
- Using good judgment with financial decisions and coping with stress in everyday life.

Why Is Impulse Control Important?

It is necessary to achieve impulse control because it helps maintain healthy relationships, regulates your behavior, empowers you to consider the consequences of your actions, engage in strategic planning, and resist the temptation to succumb to every impulse. Someone could avoid getting into legal trouble from reckless driving—such as harming others on the road, speeding tickets, accidents, etc.—by having impulse control. Impulse control can also be used to maintain positive relationships at home and school because it helps you control your emotions, be patient, and listen to others without interrupting. The consequences are much higher as you grow older.

Ways You Can Improve Your Sudden Impulses

Here are some ways to assist you in enhancing your impulse control:

1. Practice and Rehearse Alternative Behaviors

You don't just learn self-control through exercises. It is also necessary to carry out and practice the behavior that helps you stop your impulsive behaviors. You can practice impulse control skills in front of a mirror by role-playing with a friend, family member, or in private.

A. Role Play

Have the situation you are facing in mind. Visualize yourself showing self-control over your impulses while dealing with this situation. Next, consider practicing these skills with a friend or family member who can take on the role of an opponent, someone who might intentionally provoke impulsive reactions (e.g., classmates at school) or engage in activities that could test your self-control (e.g., sitting too close to a TV or talking during a group project). Another helpful technique is to simulate these scenarios at home by standing in front of a mirror and imagining yourself receiving guidance from a teacher or parent.

B. Role Reversal

This technique involves changing the roles of players in the situation. Instead of playing yourself, switch with another person and play your opponent, provoking your impulsive outburst. Then take on the other player's role and resist your impulses.

2. Pay Attention to What Triggers You

Impulsive behavior can be a defense mechanism to mask your negative feelings. Recognizing your emotions and how they influence your behaviors can help you better control impulses. Keep a daily log of your impulsive behaviors, thoughts, feelings, or urges. Then you can see which triggers most often lead to impulsive behavior. You can use those triggers to improve impulse control.

3. Use Visual Reminders

Visual reminders are an effective and practical tool for improving impulse control because you can easily carry visual reminders with you. A visual reminder is a picture, object, or written phrase that reminds you of the goal of regulating your impulses by interrupting them before they are carried out. For example, if you usually impulsively talk or text during a conversation, carry a photo of someone being quiet and calm in conversation with you. Keep one visual reminder on your desk at school or carry one in your backpack that reminds you how to say no when you feel pressured to spend money on things that aren't important (e.g., buying new clothes).

The most common visual reminders are flashing lights, symbols, and pictures. You can also move small objects with your fingers, like a small bell, or tap twice on your chest with your figure to use as memory cues.

4. Learn from the People around You

You can learn from the people around you or the people educating you. For example, how do adults cope with anger or impulsivity? How do they respond when they are around you? By observing the behaviors and actions of others, you can learn new strategies to gain insights into how different approaches could have improved your situation.

Identifying the specific issue and considering alternative approaches in hindsight is crucial because you can reflect on how you can respond differently in the future to ensure a better understanding of your intentions by others.

5. Have Good Sleep

Good sleep habits can help with impulsivity because it helps you feel refreshed and keeps you from feeling tired, angry, and stressed. Impulsive actions are increased when you're stressed or tired compared to when you are rested. Good sleep habits promote healthier eating habits and regular exercise, which means you will feel more rested and less stressed. Additionally, sleep requires adequate time and peace. This allows your body to go through the natural stages of sleep without being disturbed by environmental factors such as light or noise and overall health and well-being. So, adhere to a schedule that allows your body sufficient time to rest each night.

6. Choose Healthy Lifestyle

Healthy eating habits, including controlled diet and exercise, can improve impulse control through mood stabilization, physical relaxation, and boosted energy levels. A whole grain and vegetable diet can aid weight management, enhancing impulsivity and overall health by increasing self-esteem and reducing stress.

Exercise is another way to improve impulse control and overall health. Exercise is a stress-relieving activity that increases physical energy, reduces stress levels, boosts self-esteem, and improves sleep. If you wish to maintain a regular exercise routine, finding a form of physical activity you genuinely enjoy is the key.

Martial arts, in particular, provide a safe environment to learn how to regulate emotions and actions and manage aggression. It promotes discipline and teaches individuals to show courtesy towards others and improve emotional control.

7. Evaluate and Learn Other Executive Function Skills

As mentioned above, impulse control is an example of executive function skills that allows you to manage your behaviors and regulate your actions. Plan development, problem-solving skills, flexibility, working memory, social skills, and emotional control are essential when working on impulsivity. So, improving other executive function skills to assist in impulse control and improve your behaviors is important so you can catch yourself before they are carried out.

If you're concerned that your problem is too significant to handle alone, discussing it with professionals can be beneficial. Talking about your thoughts, feelings, and behaviors can help you get in touch with the causes and consequences of your actions and help you develop healthier ways of behaving.

PART III

BRIDGING THE GAP

10

LOOKING AHEAD IN LIFE

A s you age, your attention shifts toward the future and envisioning your desired life. The future holds numerous changes and exciting opportunities. It might involve moving out of your parents' house, pursuing higher education in college, and potentially residing in a dormitory. To thrive independently and succeed in life, you should develop specific skills. These skills will empower you to navigate new experiences, overcome challenges, and make the most of the opportunities that come your way. You want to avoid leaving things up to fate or luck because then you might end up doing something unexpected and experience restrictions exposed by others on your life. Even though this is scary, it's a natural part of growing up. It typically entails greater independence, freedom, and responsibilities, all of which are attainable if you take the time to prepare for adulthood.

PREPARING FOR THE FUTURE

As a teenager with ADHD transitioning into adulthood, one of the most intimidating moments in life can be the first time you venture out on your own. The prospect of facing unfamiliar responsibilities and challenges can feel overwhelming. You may grapple with impulsive decision-making, heightened impatience, and inappropriate reactions to everyday demands. However, being prepared and equipped to confidently navigate the real world and make informed choices is crucial. By arming yourself with knowledge and strategies, you can approach this new phase of life with resilience and make positive decisions that align with your goals and well-being.

Learn Money Management

Before you venture out on your own or embark on your college journey, it is vital to learn money management. This is the best way to prepare for adulthood.

1. Creating a Bank Account and Managing Bill Payments

To build a solid foundation in financial management, begin by focusing on the essentials, like initiating a checking account and responsibly handling bills. It is not uncommon for young individuals to get carried away with spending and surpass their income, which can result in accumulating debts and financial obligations. Therefore, it is best to contemplate the option of opening a checking account at a local bank or credit union. This account will offer a convenient method for tracking income sources and effectively monitoring expenses. By having a checking account, you cultivate a sense of accountability, self-reliance, and command over your purchases. It is a valuable tool for acquiring knowledge in money management and taking charge of your earnings. Then, gradually save money in a dedicated savings account. By consistently saving money, you will ensure a reserve for promptly settling bills, enabling faster debt repayment. Start with the basics and contribute to household bills.

2. Start saving money for a rainy day.

To be financially ready for the future, you must start saving money as soon as possible. Starting small and developing a habit of saving money is the key. You can add a couple of dollars each month to your budget until it becomes automatic. Then, you can start increasing the amount you save every month.

Here are the steps to follow:

Step 1: Take a look at your income and expenses.

To understand your monthly income clearly, keep track of your account statements and pay stubs. Knowing how much money you make monthly can establish a budget that aligns with your financial resources. This proactive approach makes it easier to stay within your budget and manage expenses effectively.

Step 2: Grade your spending habits.

To effectively save money, start by creating a list of the things you want to save for and divide them into three categories:

a. Immediate needs:
You should immediately pay expenses such as food, gas, or mortgage.
b. Future needs
You need to learn about events or expenses like buying a new vehicle and school tuition.
c. Future wants
You may want to buy things down the road, such as vacations or a home.

Step 3: Determine the size of your savings fund.

To calculate the required savings amount, begin by multiplying your monthly income by twelve to estimate your annual income. Then, divide this annual income by three to determine how much you should allocate for monthly savings. To calculate the ideal balance for your monthly savings account, multiply this monthly savings amount by twenty percent. This calculation can guide setting aside a portion of your earnings towards monthly savings.

Step 4: Set your goals.

Now that you clearly understand the monthly savings target and the designated amount for savings, it's time to set your goals and start saving. It is crucial to take charge of your finances before they become overwhelming or burdened with excessive bills. The earlier you prepare, the better equipped you'll be to make wise financial decisions. By managing your money effectively and starting your savings journey now, you pave the way for a more secure and financially sound future. Staying organized is part of a healthy financial life style.

3. Deal with credit cards responsibly.

Credit should not be a concern solely in adulthood; it is vital to be mindful of it from the moment you begin earning income. Recognizing the importance of your credit score is paramount for your future. A good credit score is necessary to borrow loans for future investments like a home, vehicle, or education. A higher score enhances your likelihood of loan approval and a better interest rate. It is crucial to prioritize promptly repaying debts to prevent accruing additional financial obligations. By establishing responsible financial practices early on, you pave the way for success when making substantial purchases.

4. Track of your money.

Learn how to create a budget plan to effectively manage your monthly income and expenses to avoid overspending and poor financial decisions in your early years of adulthood. This knowledge empowers you to recognize areas of potential overspending and make appropriate modifications to stay within your budget.

You can use ledgers and spreadsheets to track your expenses and income. Use your debit and credit cards wisely. If you can't afford something, don't buy it.

Another useful strategy is establishing an automatic withdrawal plan from your checking account for fixed expenses. You can streamline the payment process by consolidating your credit card debt into one monthly payment. This approach simplifies your financial obligations and ensures you make fewer monthly payments rather than juggling multiple payments.

You can also use money-tracking apps on your mobile device to manage your finances and record all purchases and expenses. By implementing these practices, you gain greater control over your finances and can make informed decisions to achieve your financial goals.

5. Find a way to have fun without breaking the bank.

Discover ways to enjoy yourself without spending too much money, such as going to a movie at a cheaper time, hiking with friends, or hanging out at a local coffee shop. Additionally, there are numerous activities you can engage in that don't require spending any money, like playing a sport, reading a book, going for a walk, spending time at home with family, or watching your favorite show.

Being frugal requires creativity and the ability to maximize resources. Consider the following strategies to save money:

a. Shop around.

When it comes to groceries or clothing, don't settle for the first option you find. Take the opportunity to compare prices and visit various retailers. Online platforms and local stores can offer different deals and discounts, allowing you to make informed choices and maximize the value of your money.

b. Buy used items.

Buying used items can be smart since there are used items online at affordable prices but in excellent condition. The difference is that you must be careful when purchasing used items from unknown sellers on websites such as Facebook marketplace. You should inspect used items before purchasing.

c. Cook at home.

Cooking at home is a money-saving strategy. You can save money by creating new recipes and buying the ingredients beforehand.

d. Use coupons/promotions to get discounts.

Other methods of saving money include using promotions or coupons when shopping. When you go to the supermarket, look through weekly circulars or websites to find digital coupons. Before purchasing, it's wise to explore different stores to find the best deal and save as much money as possible. You can get the most value for your hard-earned money by checking out multiple options.

e. Sell or donate things that you don't need or want anymore.

Suppose you find yourself no longer needing or interested in an item. In that case, you may want to explore the option of selling it or donating it to a charitable organization such as Goodwill. There are also charitable organizations that offer free items or guidance on donations.

f. Plan your shopping so that you only buy what you need.

To save money while shopping, plan your purchases to avoid getting stuck with unwanted items and finish shopping so they all fit into one shopping trip instead of buying one thing at a time.

g. Buy in bulk, but don't impulsively buy.

Bulk shopping can effectively save money since you can get discounts for buying in bulk. You should use your items responsibly so that you don't go through the items quickly and have to buy more, which will add up the costs again.

h. Stop using credit cards for all but necessities.

A credit card can be useful when purchasing expensive items but should not be used for other purposes. Even if you pay off your credit card monthly, using it for everyday purchases can rack up interest charges and put you in debt. Using cash or debit cards for all your purchases can be a good idea. Another option is to pay off your credit cards every month.

Saving money can be challenging as it demands discipline and careful planning. Nonetheless, it is one of the most effective ways to ensure a financially secure future. Being frugal doesn't mean living in poverty; it means finding ways to save while still enjoying life. By practicing frugality and learning to live within a budget from a young age, you can transform your financial habits and establish a solid foundation for a prosperous future.

6. Request assistance if you need it!

You are never alone in your journey —there is always someone willing to help you. If you need assistance finding a job, ask your parents, siblings, relatives, or close friends for help.

Don't let financial concerns overshadow your enjoyment of life. While ADHD symptoms can pose challenges, you can still achieve your goals of saving and having fun. Striking a balance between spending and frugality is key to finding financial satisfaction.

HOW TO COPE IN THE REAL WORLD

As you venture into the real world, your parents won't be able to do certain things for you. Learning things on your own is necessary. Living in the real-world means you must become an adult and be responsible for yourself. Becoming a fully independent grown-up will take time, but you can start learning NOW.

Here are some key points to consider:

1. Take Your Medication as Prescribed.

Your parents might have reminded you about your medications, but when you move out and get a job, you must be responsible for getting your prescriptions.

2. Learn to do housework.

Learning essential life skills such as doing dishes, laundry, cleaning, vacuuming, and cooking is important for your future independence. It's a good idea to observe and learn from your parents or guardians as they perform these tasks, paying close attention to their techniques. By developing these skills now, you'll be better prepared to handle these responsibilities in the future.

202 | LEILA MOLAIE

3. Get a job and learn self-discipline.

In the real world, only the strong can survive. You must learn to be responsible early in life and get a job. A job will teach valuable life skills and make you more reliable, dependable, and accountable. You can start by searching online or applying to your state's vocational rehabilitation services.

4. Become a better driver.

It would be advantageous if you learned how to drive to easily commute to school and work. Being a good driver will also save you money by getting less expensive insurance, not paying for tickets, paying to fix and repair your car due to auto accidents, and, more importantly, you will be safe.

5. Stay away from alcohol and drugs.

Living in the real world is intimidating, and you might feel tempted to try alcohol or drugs. You might even have friends who pressure you to accompany them. Don't try these substances if they are illegal in your state, addictive, or impair your senses from operating to your full capacity. It is important to understand that some of your symptoms, such as distractibility, hyperactivity, and impulsivity, might worsen if you abuse alcohol or drugs. Educate yourself about the risks and effects of alcohol and drugs.

6. Figure out how to deal with ADHD symptoms better.

When you live alone in the real world, certain things might bother you more than when your parents were around. You may get distracted more often or get frustrated. You will probably have to work hard until you can make some changes. Facing challenges and overcoming obstacles is never easy, but it's crucial to remember that you can persevere.

Learning how to manage in the real world is a time-consuming process. When you live independently, responsibilities like doing dishes, laundry, cleaning, vacuuming, and cooking become your responsibility. Learning to do them properly now will contribute to your independence later in life. Pay close attention to how your parents or guardians do things. By acquiring these skills early on, you'll gain the necessary independence to handle household tasks without relying on others. Remember that you are maturing, preparing for adulthood, and learning what it means to be an independent adult. Don't let your ADHD get in the way of your success.

11

SELF ADVOCACY AND SELF-AWARENESS AFTER HIGH SCHOOL

S elf-advocacy is the most critical skill for college students or young adults with ADHD but is rarely taught in middle or high school. Self-advocacy skills are a set of behaviors to communicate that you have valuable skills and talents, standing up for yourself and speaking out about what you need or believe in so they can understand you better and treat you the way you expect. Self-advocacy helps you take control of your life, make the right choices, and ask for help or support when needed.

Self-advocacy is directly related to self-awareness, which can only be achieved when you know your values and beliefs, strengths, and weaknesses, and how you interact with people in meaningful contexts such as school, friends, family, and peers. Staying calm and

206 | LEILA MOLAIE

composed in challenging situations is important. It may also require developing a tolerance for taking risks and standing up for your rights, regardless of the potential consequences.

SELF-AWARENESS ACTIVITIES

1. Create a success file

Write a "Success File" to record your daily achievements. Success is not defined by grades but by demonstrating that you believe in yourself as an individual with self-worth and are willing to take risks to achieve your goals. Add tasks you feel confident you could accomplish if you wanted to but put them in the "Do" column and tasks you're not confident about in the "Don't" column. Begin cross-referencing the two categories to identify patterns that indicate whether you are progressing toward your goals and aspirations.

2. Develop a personal self-advocacy plan

Consider the following steps to reach your personal goals:

- Identify your goals, such as "start a business," "learn a new language," or "travel the world."

- Complete the paragraph: "I **want to achieve** my goal(s) because

  _____."

- Brainstorm a list of actions you can take to achieve each goal. Be as specific as possible.
- Reflect on how you can support yourself in reaching these goals. Consider what resources, skills, or knowledge you already have and what you need to acquire.
- Determine how others can contribute to your goals. Think about individuals who can provide guidance, mentorship, or practical assistance.
- Identify any behaviors or actions from others that may hinder your progress and make a note to address those issues.
- Assess your habits and behaviors. Identify any actions not aligned with your goals and commit to stopping them.
- Take a short break to recharge and refocus.

Review your list and prioritize the actions that can be immediately implemented. Take the first step towards your goals.

Review and adjust your plan daily to stay on track. Stay committed, motivated, and open to trying different approaches. You can make significant progress toward achieving your goals with determination and perseverance.

3. Create a Situational Action Plan (SAP)

The Situational Action Plan (SAP) is a planning tool developed to focus on specific situations you might encounter while pursuing your dreams. Write down goals, positive behaviors, and negative behaviors. Planning helps you prepare and manage your emotions to handle stressful situations effectively. You can use SAP by writing down a situation that is likely to occur. Then, write down positive and negative items under it. For example, the positive thing might be, "talk with my advisor about what I want to do for my major," "go to class," or "feel successful after class." And for the negative items, write things that you might do that can get in the way of your goal fulfillment. So, you might say, "feel frustrated over having to do this," "expect too much of myself," or "get frustrated when I am feeling overwhelmed by classes and friends."

4. Keep a journal

Keeping a journal is an effective way to track your goals and personal development. By documenting your daily experiences, both positive and negative, you gain valuable insights into your emotions, relationships, and progress. Reflect on your feelings, the people involved, and the outcomes of different situations. While journaling daily is unnecessary, ensure consistency and make it a regular practice. Writing about your life prompts introspection, helping you assess satisfaction and identify areas for improvement. Additionally, it provides feedback on your goal pursuit and self-advocacy journey.

5. Learn from your mistakes

This exercise provides a valuable opportunity to gain awareness of your surroundings, take appropriate action, and evaluate their impact on your goals. There is no absolute right or wrong in this process. By considering the ideas generated in the previous exercise, clarity will emerge. Reflecting on recent weeks or months may reveal recurring patterns and familiar challenges to prevent issues from escalating beyond control.

6. Set up a support system

Having a support system is invaluable when it comes to achieving your goals. The individuals within this network offer encouragement, guidance, and help to set realistic expectations. Additionally, they provide emotional support throughout your journey.

Connecting with others who share the same interest and are pursuing similar goals can be inspiring and comforting.

If you're seeking someone to discuss your goals with, consider utilizing online resources, message boards, or support groups. These platforms connect you with like-minded individuals, whether finding groups focused on relevant topics or connecting with individuals with similar backgrounds and professional aspirations. Through experimentation, you can discover which methods work best for you.

ADHD AFTER HIGH SCHOOL

Considering college as an option after high school is a significant decision that can shape your future. However, it is important to acknowledge that navigating college with ADHD can present challenges. The academic expectations, pressure to succeed, and potential distractions can sometimes feel overwhelming, causing you to feel pulled in different directions.

Why You Should Not Rush College

Contrary to the belief that entering college immediately after high school increases chances of success, this may not be true for everyone, including those with

ADHD. Rushing into college without thoughtful consideration may not always be beneficial, regardless of whether you have ADHD. It is crucial to weigh all options and make a well-informed decision about pursuing higher education.

Factors You Need to Consider

1. Financial aid

Considering financial aid is a crucial aspect when planning for college. Many colleges require students to apply for financial aid to access federal or state grants and federal loans. However, it's important to note that financial aid is not guaranteed, and the application process can be time-consuming and stressful. It is essential to approach the financial aid process with realistic expectations and understand that it may not provide a complete solution, requiring additional financial planning and consideration.

2. Stress, anxiety, and motivation

Alongside financial aid, it is crucial to consider your stress levels when contemplating college attendance. Managing stress plays a significant role in your motivation and overall college experience. It can be challenging to navigate emotions directly, especially if you're not used to doing so. Feelings of being overwhelmed, impostor syndrome, or self-doubt may arise.

It is important to prioritize self-care, maintain a positive attitude, and cultivate a sense of self-worth throughout college. Additionally, seeking support from friends, family, or campus resources can be beneficial in managing stress and maintaining a healthy mindset.

3. ADHD versus thoughts of failure

When you have ADHD, it can be challenging to switch gears in college. You are accustomed to doing things at your own pace; going back and forth between work and school is hard. However, by employing the appropriate techniques, you can feel better prepared for these transitions and have a more enjoyable time while attending college.

4. Meeting standards

To succeed in college, you must put in much effort. College admissions committees wish for someone who will work hard and contribute to their school. As someone with ADHD, it can be hard for you to show these qualities because of your natural tendency towards procrastination and avoidance of tasks related to school or work. It is essential to establish specific objectives and focus on areas requiring improvement.

5. Personality traits

You are an individual with particular interests and dislikes. You should identify these areas to choose your major. Those who rush to get into college often do not spend time exploring their options, learning about the work market, and identifying in-demand occupations. On the other hand, college admissions committees prioritize finding individuals who align well with their institution. You can teach yourself ways to excel in this setting and become more confident about yourself, thus finding the right school and a good major, and improving your chances of admission.

These reasons are not to deter you from going to college but to ensure you do your research before deciding on your next steps. It is best to take your time to make the right decision.

How to Succeed with ADHD After High School

1. Ensure academic success.

When you achieve academic success, you will have a higher sense of self-worth and enter the workforce with greater assurance. Before each semester, meet with a counselor from the Disability Services of your college and request an accommodation. The key is to apply before or as soon as you register for your classes. These accommodations can include extra time, multiple breaks during the exam, recording the sessions, using a calculator, etc.

2. Identify your skills and passions.

Discovering your skills and passions can be time-consuming, but it is ultimately rewarding for your future endeavors. First, assess your high school records and seek input from teachers who have evaluated your performance to help narrow down your interests. While it's natural to have multiple passions and interests, it's crucial to prioritize and concentrate on one at a time. Select your primary interest, take small steps to begin, and commit yourself to refine your skills and talents as you work towards your objectives.

3. Build skills.

Consider enrolling in after-school or summer activities that align with your interests. Explore options like art classes, community theater groups, music lessons, or joining your school's athletics team. These activities provide opportunities for personal growth and promote acceptance and leadership. Keep in mind that pursuing these endeavors requires dedication and commitment.

4. Expose yourself to career options.

Explore a variety of careers that may pique your interest. Start with an area you enjoy and find career options that fit your passions. You can also register at community colleges, attend programs and workshops that provide knowledge in your chosen area of interest, or join a local professional organization. Attend career fairs to learn about different companies and meet people who can help guide you into the field of work you want to pursue.

5. Request transition services.

Discuss available transition services with your school's child study team or transition coordinator to learn about community programs. Most schools have in-school transition programs or outreach job coaching services to offer job shadowing, job sampling, or placement services. Ensure you are referred to or have applied to your state's Vocational Rehabilitation Services (VRS). These services are often available to students with Individualized Educational Plans (IEP) or 504 plans as soon as the students turn fourteen. Each VRS state agency offers students a wide range of services, including:

- Job Exploration Counselling
- Instruction in self-advocacy skills

- Work-based learning experiences
- Counseling for enrollment opportunities at Institutions of Higher Education (IHE)
- Workplace readiness training

These VRS agencies can offer vocational counseling and guidance in addition to financial support to attend training programs or offer coaching services after high school if the individuals are willing and committed to reaching successful employment outcomes.

6. Request a career interest inventory.

Both high schools and colleges provide various resources for career exploration, including formal career interest inventories and online assessments. One such assessment is the Strong Interest Inventory (available at themyersbriggs.com), which uses questions about your preferences to determine your work personality and suggests specific professions that align with your characteristics. These inventories can be valuable tools for initiating discussions with teachers and counselors, helping you gain insights into your career interests and possibilities.

7. Consider job shadowing.

Job shadowing offers a valuable opportunity to observe a job firsthand before committing to it. Approach someone currently working in your desired field and asks if you can spend a few days observing them. Prepare a list of questions to ask them about the job such as its responsibilities, salary, required education, relevant courses, and the type of people one works with. This experience will provide insights into the job's reality and help determine if it aligns with your long-term goals. Afterward, reflect on what you learned and how it influences your plans. Also, you can contact your school transition coordinator or VRS agencies for placement services.

8. Apply for summer jobs.

Spring is the time to begin exploring potential summer job opportunities, which can serve to gain insights into various career fields and make money. Consider reaching out to local businesses or organizations to inquire about available positions. Focus on developing new skills and increasing self-confidence, as these factors contribute to long-term success beyond obtaining a diploma. Take a moment to reflect and define what success means to you. Consider the type of work and lifestyle that aligns with your passions, brings you joy, and fulfills you.

LEAVE A 1-CLICK REVIEW!

I would be incredibly thankful if you could take 60 seconds to write a brief review on Amazon, even if it is just a few sentences!

Customer reviews

 5 out of 5

2 global ratings

5 star		100%
4 star		0%
3 star		0%
2 star		0%
1 star		0%

˅ How customer reviews and ratings work

You can also send me your feedback and questions using my email:

higherself@mobiagroup.com

CONCLUSION

This two-volume book on ADHD in adolescence provides a comprehensive guide to help young adults with ADHD overcome the challenges they face in various aspects of their lives. The first volume laid the foundation by discussing signs, symptoms, treatment options, and managing emotions. It emphasized the importance of managing emotions, understanding the treatment options available, and how individuals with ADHD can use their unique strengths to their advantage.

The second volume builds on this knowledge by providing practical strategies and tools to help young adults with ADHD develop social skills, improve executive function, manage their time better, enhance their memory, control their impulses, and planning for adult life. It also guides them through the challenging transition from adolescence to adulthood and helps them plan for their future.

I acknowledge the challenges that individuals with ADHD and their families face. However, I am confident that with proper support and effective strategies, young adults with ADHD can reach their maximum potential and excel in various aspects of life.

I strongly encourage families and young adults with ADHD to embrace the techniques and strategies outlined in this book. Integrating these practices into their daily routines can enhance their social skills, improve executive function, optimize time management, enhance learning and retention, regulate impulses, and effectively plan for their future. I believe that with hard work, perseverance, and the right support, individuals with ADHD can overcome their challenges and lead fulfilling and successful lives. By incorporating the techniques and strategies presented in this book, they can navigate the challenges of ADHD successfully and achieve their full potential.

I truly hope you find as much joy and enlightenment in this book as I have and that it has provided fresh insights and perspectives. You deserve a life filled with contentment and happiness, and I am committed to supporting you in achieving that.

I would love your reflections on this book's methods, ideas, and discoveries. Your feedback and thoughts are valuable to me. Consider it a minor exercise in concentration, planning, and task initiation, and then post a review on Amazon describing how this book benefited you. I'm most curious to know how you plan to use the techniques and ideas discussed here and whether they were as successful for you as they were for others.

REFERENCES

8 reasons why working memory is important—Edublox online tutor. (2022, April 14). https://www.edubloxtutor.com/8-reasons-why-working-memory-is-important/

ADDitude editors. (2022, March 31). *Everyday add stigmas: Enduring adhd myths and stereotypes.* Additude. https://www.additudemag.com/adhd-stereotypes-add-stigma/

ADDitude Editors. (2022, July 22). *Positives of adhd: 12 amazing superpowers.* Additude. https://www.additudemag.com/slideshows/positives-of-adhd/

Adhd. (n.d.). Psychology Today. https://www.psychologytoday.com/us/basics/adhd

Adhd executive function and school success – add resource center. (2012, June 6). https://www.addrc.org/executive-function-and-school-success/

ADHD in children. (n.d.). Psychology.Org; Australian Psychological Society. https://psychology.org.au/for-the-public/psychology-topics/adhd-in-children

Adhd teens and relationship problems. (n.d.). Healthyplace. https://www.healthyplace.com/adhd/articles/adhd-teens-and-relationship-problems

Arain, M., Haque, M., Johal, L., Mathur, P., Nel, W., Rais, A., Sandhu, R., & Sharma, S. (2012). Maturation of the adolescent brain. *Neuropsychiatric Disease and Treatment, 9,* 449-461. https://doi.org/10.2147/NDT.S39776

Attention-deficit/hyperactivity disorder, children. (n.d.). Psychology Today. https://www.psychologytoday.com/us/conditions/attention-deficit-hyperactivity-disorder-children

Attention-deficit/hyperactivity disorder, teen. (n.d.). Psychology Today. https://www.psychologytoday.com/us/conditions/attention-deficit-hyperactivity-disorder-teen

Azab, M. (2019, September 8). *A non-medicinal treatment for adhd and why it works.* Psychology Today. https://www.psychologytoday. com/us/blog/neuroscience-in-everyday-life/201909/non-medici nal-treatment-adhd-and-why-it-works

Belsky, G. (n.d.-a). *Adhd treatment options.* Understood. https://www. understood.org/en/articles/treatment-for-kids-with-adhd

Belsky, G. (n.d.-b). *Cognitive behavioral therapy: What is cbt?* Understood. https://www.understood.org/en/articles/faqs-about-cognitive-behavioral-therapy

Belsky, G. (n.d.-c). *Types of executive function skills.* Understood. https:// www.understood.org/en/articles/types-of-executive-function-skills

Belsky, G. (n.d.-d). *What is executive function?* Understood. https:// www.understood.org/en/articles/what-is-executive-function

Benefits of adhd / add: Love your strengths and abilities. (2022, June 24). Additude. https://www.additudemag.com/slideshows/benefits-of-adhd-to-love/

Benisek, A. (2021, April 9). *Adhd in children: Focus on the positives.* WebMD. https://www.webmd.com/add-adhd/childhood-adhd/features/focus-on-positives

Beresin, D. M. N.-V. and D. G. (2017, February 6). *The adolescent brain: Why executive functioning in teens is a challenge.* https://www.beyond booksmart.com/executive-functioning-strategies-blog/the-adoles cent-brain-why-executive-functioning-in-teens-is-a-challenge

Bernstein, S. (2021, November 13). *Adhd and your emotions: Tips to help you manage them.* WebMD. https://www.webmd.com/add-adhd/emotion-stress

Bertin, M. (2019, August 12). *Mindfulness, adhd, and emotion: A natural and practical fit.* Psychology Today. https://www.psychologytoday. com/us/blog/child-development-central/201908/mindfulness-adhd-and-emotion-natural-and-practical-fit

Better time management for teens—Help them, help yourself. (n.d.). Time Management Success. https://www.time-management-success. com/time-management-for-teens.html

Brady, C. (2022, February 17). *How to make friends: Social skills for teens with adhd.* https://www.additudemag.com/social-skills-teens-adhd-high-school/

Bransford, J.D. & Stein, B.S. (1984). The IDEAL Problem Solver, A guide for improving thinking, learning, and creativity. 2nd edition. W. H. Freeman and Company

Breaux, R. (2020). Emotion regulation in teens with adhd. *CHADD.* https://chadd.org/adhd-news/adhd-news-caregivers/emotion-regulation-in-teens-with-adhd/

Brown, T. (n.d.). *How adhd and executive function challenges are related.* Understood. https://www.understood.org/en/articles/relation ship-between-adhd-andexecutive-function-challenges

CDC. (2020, September 21). *Treatment of adhd.* Centers for Disease Control and Prevention. https://www.cdc.gov/ncbddd/adhd/treatment.html

Common adhd medications & treatments for children. (2022, October 20). HealthyChildren.Org. https://www.healthychildren.org/English/health-issues/conditions/adhd/Pages/Determining-ADHD-Medication-Treatments.aspx

Cronkleton, E. (2021, August 13). *ADHD brain vs. normal brain: Function, differences, and more.* Medical News Today. https://www.medicalnewstoday.com/articles/adhd-brain-vs-normal-brain

Daily management of adhd. (n.d.). Psychology Today. https://www.psychologytoday.com/us/basics/adhd/daily-management-adhd

Dandy, C. (2021, April 5). *What to do after high school: A guide for teens with adhd.* Additude. https://www.additudemag.com/what-to-do-after-high-school/

disabilitydc. (n.d.). Disability dc. *Tumblr.* https://disabilitydc.tumblr.com/post/172918636647/bart-and-wally-both-have-adhd-which-helps-them

Division of developmental disabilities. (n.d.). https://www.nj.gov/humanservices/ddd/

Do adhd 'super powers' exist? (n.d.). Kennedy Krieger Institute. https://www.kennedykrieger.org/stories/making-difference/inspiring-stories/do-adhd-super-powers-exist

Dodson, W. (2022, August 24). *Adhd brain: Unraveling secrets of your add nervous system.* Additude. https://www.additudemag.com/secrets-of-the-adhd-brain/

Dunbar, K. (2017). Problem Solving. 289-298. https://doi.org/10. 1002/9781405164535.ch20

Dupar, L. (2019, August 11). *Did You Know that Having ADHD is Like Having Super Powers?* IACTcenter. https://www.iactcenter.com/ adhd-super-powers/

Elmaghraby, R., & Garayalde, S. (2022, June). *What Is ADHD?* Psychiatry.Org; American Psychiatric Association.

Estante, R. (2015, September 20). *An Interview with Dr. Julie Schweitzer – Part I.* Adda. https://add.org/an-interview-with-dr-julie-schweitzer-part-i-2/

Retrieved from: https://mantracare.org/therapy/what-is/expressing-yourself/

Fiery, R. (2022, November 2). *What are my teen's options after high school?* Additude. https://www.additudemag.com/adhd-teen-options-after-high-school/

Finch, S. D. (2020, August 31). *Adhd quick tips: 11 focus boosts when your brain won't cooperate.* Healthline. https://www.healthline.com/ health/mental-health/adhd-quick-focus-boosts

Five ways to improve emotional regulation. (2020, June 22). *Next Step 4 ADHD.* https://www.nextstep4adhd.com/five-ways-to-improve-emotional-regulation/

Foley, D. (n.d.). The truth about adhd. *TIME.Com.* https://time.com/ growing-up-with-adhd/

Gap year: Using a "nap" year to recharge my child with adhd. (2019, December 18). https://www.additudemag.com/gap-year-for-adhd-teens-before-college/

Hallowell, E., & Ratey, J. (2005, July 12). *Excerpt: "delivered from distraction."* NPR. https://www.npr.org/2005/07/12/4749307/excerpt-delivered-from-distraction

Johnson, J. (2021, May 18). *Can exercise help treat ADHD?* Medical News Today. https://www.medicalnewstoday.com/articles/adhd-cardio

junecao. (2021, March 3). 11 skills to help your teen with adhd. *Mind Connections.* https://mindconnectionsnyc.com/11-skills-to-help-your-teen-with-adhd/

Kelly, K. (n.d.-a). *Adhd alternative treatment.* Understood. https://www. understood.org/en/articles/adhd-alternative-treatment-what-you-need-to-know

Kelly, K. (n.d.-b). *Tips for executive function challenges in everyday life.* Understood. https://www.understood.org/en/articles/everyday-challenges-with-executive-function

Kingsley, E. (2022, March 31). *Adhd stigma at school: Support and stories.* Additude. https://www.additudemag.com/adhd-stigma-at-school/

Koppert, J. (2020, November 16). *Why is ADHD so discriminated against and how can we overcome the stigma?* Indy100 Conversations. https:// conversations.indy100.com/adhd-awareness-disability-stigma

Lovering, N. (2022, April 21). *Adhd stigma: Breaking the silence.* Psych Central. https://psychcentral.com/adhd/breaking-the-silence-of-adhd-stigma

Low, K. (2021, April 12). *Understanding anger in children with adhd.* Verywell Mind. https://www.verywellmind.com/understanding-adhd-children-and-anger-20540

Low, K. (2022, April 22). *What it's like for kids with adhd.* Verywell Mind. https://www.verywellmind.com/understanding-children-with-adhd-20686

Ma, L. (2017, April 4). *What we've learned about adhd.* Psychology Today. https://www.psychologytoday.com/us/blog/brainstorm/201704/what-weve-learned-about-adhd

McGuire, C. (2022, October 28). *How to improve social skills in children with adhd: Tips for parents.* Additude. https://www.additudemag. com/how-to-improve-social-skills-adhd-children/

Marla. (2020, July 17). The 5 tips adhd adults need to effectively reduce overwhelm. *Marla Cummins.* https://marlacummins.com/adhd-overwhelm/

Marla. (2022, November 14). Adhd adults communicate better using these 7 listening tips. *Marla Cummins.* https://marlacummins.com/adhd-adults-and-challenges-listening/

Michaels, P., Gilbert , P., Frye, D., & Rodden, J. (2022, March 31). *Brain Training for ADHD: What Is It? Does It Work?* Additude. https://www. additudemag.com/adhd-brain-training-neurofeedback-memory/

Morin, A. (n.d.-a). *7 ways to teach your high-schooler organization skills*. Understood. https://www.understood.org/en/articles/at-a-glance-7-ways-to-teach-your-high-schooler-organization-skills

Morin, A. (n.d.-b). *8 common myths about adhd*. https://www.understood.org/en/articles/common-myths-about-adhd

Morin, A. (n.d.-c). *Adhd and social skills*. Understood. https://www.understood.org/en/articles/5-ways-adhd-can-affect-social-skills

Muller, R. (2015, June 10). *Distinct adhd symptoms in girls result in under-diagnosis*. Psychology Today. https://www.psychologytoday.com/us/blog/talking-about-trauma/201506/distinct-adhd-symptoms-in-girls-result-in-under-diagnosis

Myths and misunderstandings. (n.d.). *CHADD*. https://chadd.org/about-adhd/myths-and-misunderstandings/

Nall, R. (2021, January 19). *Why having adhd can be a benefit*. Healthline. https://www.healthline.com/health/adhd/benefits-of-adhd

Ohwovoriole, T. (2022, July 9). *The three adhd subtypes and how to recognize them*. Verywell Mind. https://www.verywellmind.com/how-to-recognize-the-three-adhd-subtypes-5089419

Organization skills for students: 7 practical tips. (2018, March 21). https://www.schoolplanner.com/organization-skills-students/

Patino, E. (n.d.). *Social skills groups for children | social skills training for adhd*. Understood. https://www.understood.org/en/articles/faqs-about-social-skills-groups

Pay attention to distracted Da Vincis; naughty kids who tap their feet impatiently may well be the next. (2019, May 27). *The Economic Times*. https://economictimes.indiatimes.com/magazines/panache/pay-attention-to-distracted-da-vincis-naughty-kids-who-tap-their-feet-impatiently-may-well-be-the-next/articleshow/69511909.cms

Ph.D, G. L. (2021, May 21). *Social skills training for adults: 10 best activities + pdf*. PositivePsychology.Com. https://positivepsychology.com/social-skills-training/

Pomodoro Technique. (2023, February 10). In Wikipedia. https://en.wikipedia.org/wiki/Pomodoro_Technique

Porter, E. (2022, May 6). *Learn the triggers for your adhd symptoms*.

Healthline. https://www.healthline.com/health/adhd/adhd-trigger-symptoms

Preparing your teenager with adhd to move out for the first time. (n.d.). Study.Com. https://study.com/blog/preparing-your-teenager-with-adhd-to-move-out-for-the-first-time.html

Rastogi, R., Arora, N., Tawar, P. S. (2018). Statistical Analysis for Effect of Positive Thinking on Stress Management and Creative Problem Solving for Adolescents. *International Conference on "Computing for Sustainable Global Development".*

Rawe, J. (n.d.-a). *How adhd medication works in the brain.* Understood. https://www.understood.org/en/articles/how-adhd-medication-works

Rawe, J. (n.d.-b). *The adhd brain.* Understood. https://www.understood.org/en/articles/adhd-and-the-brain

Reed, P. (2019, June 22). *Does excessive screen time cause adhd?* Psychology Today. https://www.psychologytoday.com/us/blog/digital-world-real-world/201906/does-excessive-screen-time-cause-adhd

Relationships & social skills. (n.d.). *CHADD.* https://chadd.org/for-adults/relationships-social-skills/

Rettew, D. (2015, March 19). Is adhd genetically influenced? Yes! *Psychology Today.* https://www.psychologytoday.com/us/blog/abcs-child-psychiatry/201503/is-adhd-genetically-influenced-yes

Rettew, D. (2018, May 7). *Adhd is real: Brain differences in preschool-age children.* Psychology Today. https://www.psychologytoday.com/us/blog/abcs-child-psychiatry/201805/adhd-is-real-brain-differences-in-preschool-age-children

Rodden, J., Nigg, J., & Additude Editors. (2022, September 20). *Impulsivity and the adhd brain: Neural networks, explained!* Additude. https://www.additudemag.com/adhd-brain-impulsivity-explained/

Roggli, L. (2021, June 7). *Adhd communication skills: Watch your words to become an effective speaker.* Additude. https://www.additudemag.com/watch-your-words-how-adhders-can-become-great-communicators/

Saline, S. (2022, February 3). *Adhd and self-awareness | psychology today.*

https://www.psychologytoday.com/us/blog/your-way-adhd/202202/adhd-and-self-awareness

Schultz, J. (2021, December 13). *What is self-awareness? How to teach self-advocacy skills to adhd kids.* Additude. https://www.additudemag.com/self-awareness-activities-self-advocacy-skills-adhd/

Self-monitoring. (n.d.). *LD@school.* https://www.ldatschool.ca/learning-modules/executive-functions/eight-pillars/self-monitoring/

Sherman, C. (2022, September 12). *Overcoming adhd stigma: Emotions and shame.* Additude. https://www.additudemag.com/overcoming-adhd-stigma/

Sherman, C., Ramsay, R., & Barrow, K. (2022, July 13). *Cbt for adhd: Cognitive behavioral therapy for add symptoms.* Additude. https://www.additudemag.com/cognitive-behavioral-therapy-for-adhd/

Sherrell, Z. (2021, July 21). *What are the benefits of ADHD?* Medical News Today. https://www.medicalnewstoday.com/articles/adhd-benefits

Silver, L. & Additude Editors. (2022, September 21). *The adhd brain: Neuroscience behind attention deficit disorder.* Additude. https://www.additudemag.com/neuroscience-of-adhd-brain/

Sinfield, J. (2022, November 14). *The adhd vs. Non-adhd brain.* Verywell Mind. https://www.verywellmind.com/the-adhd-brain-4129396

Sippl, A. (2020a, July 9). *Executive functioning skills 101: The basics of planning | life skills advocate.* https://lifeskillsadvocate.com/blog/executive-functioning-skills-101-the-basics-of-planning/

Sippl, A. (2020b, July 23). *10 planning skills every child should learn | life skills advocate.* https://lifeskillsadvocate.com/blog/10-planning-skills-every-child-should-learn/

Sippl, A. (2020c, August 20). *Executive functioning skills 101: Time management | life skills advocate.* https://lifeskillsadvocate.com/blog/executive-functioning-skills-101-the-basics-of-time-management/

Sippl, A. (2020d, September 3). *12 time management skills to teach your child now | life skills advocate.* https://lifeskillsadvocate.com/blog/12-time-management-skills-to-teach-your-child-now/

Sippl, A. (2020e, September 18). *Executive function skills by age: What to look for | life skills advocate.* https://lifeskillsadvocate.com/blog/exec utive-function-skills-by-age/

Sippl, A. (2020f, October 1). *Executive functioning skills 101: Task initiation | life skills advocate.* https://lifeskillsadvocate.com/blog/execu tive-functioning-skills-101-the-basics-of-task-initiation/

Sippl, A. (2020g, November 12). *Executive functioning skills 101: Organization | life skills advocate.* https://lifeskillsadvocate.com/blog/ executive-functioning-skills-101-all-about-organization/

Sippl, A. (2020h, December 3). *7 organization skills to teach your teen | life skills advocate.* https://lifeskillsadvocate.com/blog/7-organization-skills-to-teach-your-teen/

Sippl, A. (2020i, December 24). *Executive functioning skills 101: Problem solving | life skills advocate.* https://lifeskillsadvocate.com/blog/execu tive-functioning-skills-101-problem-solving/

Sippl, A. (2021a, January 21). *Teaching the ideal problem-solving method to diverse learners | life skills advocate.* https://lifeskillsadvocate.com/ blog/teaching-the-ideal-problem-solving-method-to-diverse-learners/

Sippl, A. (2021b, February 18). *Executive functioning skills 101: Flexibility | life skills advocate.* https://lifeskillsadvocate.com/blog/executive-functioning-skills-101-flexibility/

Sippl, A. (2021c, February 26). *7 cognitive flexibility strategies to support your adolescent | life skills advocate.* https://lifeskillsadvocate.com/blog/7-flexible-thinking-strategies-to-support-your-teen-or-young-adult/

Sippl, A. (2021d, March 18). *Executive functioning skills 101: Working memory | life skills advocate.* https://lifeskillsadvocate.com/blog/exec utive-functioning-skills-101-working-memory/

Sippl, A. (2021e, June 4). *Executive functioning skills 101: Impulse control | life skills advocate.* https://lifeskillsadvocate.com/blog/executive-functioning-101-all-about-impulse-control/

Sippl, A. (2021f, June 17). *5 ways to help your teen learn impulse control | life skills advocate.* https://lifeskillsadvocate.com/blog/5-ways-to-help-your-teen-learn-impulse-control/

Sippl, A. (2021g, July 1). *Executive functioning skills 101: Attentional control | life skills advocate*. https://lifeskillsadvocate.com/blog/execu tive-functioning-101-all-about-attentional-control/

Sippl, A. (2021h, August 5). *Executive functioning skills 101: Self-moni-toring | life skills advocate*. https://lifeskillsadvocate.com/blog/execu tive-functioning-101-all-about-self-monitoring/

State vocational rehabilitation agencies | rehabilitation services administration. (n.d.). https://rsa.ed.gov/about/states

Stickler, J. (2020, July 28). *Celebrating adhd super powers with my students*. Additude. https://www.additudemag.com/celebrating-adhd-super-powers/

The pomodoro® technique | cirillo consulting gmbh. (n.d.). https://francesco cirillo.com/products/the-pomodoro-technique

The Understood Team. (2017, April 23). *Large-scale mri study confirms adhd brain differences*. Understood. https://www.understood.org/en/articles/large-scale-mri-study-confirms-adhd-brain-differences

Trotman, J. (2021, February 1). *It's time to talk about reducing the stigma around ADHD*. NCMH. https://www.ncmh.info/2021/02/01/its-time-to-talk-about-reducing-the-stigma-around-adhd/

Understanding hypersensitivity and adhd. (n.d.). ADDept. https://www.addept.org/living-with-adult-add-adhd/how-to-understand-hyper sensitivity-in-adhd

Understood Team. (n.d.-a). *Adhd medication*. Understood. https://www.understood.org/en/articles/adhd-medication

Understood Team. (n.d.-b). *Adhd medication side effects*. Understood. https://www.understood.org/en/articles/adhd-medication-side-effects

Understood Team. (n.d.-c). *Adhd medications for children*. Understood. https://www.understood.org/en/articles/types-of-adhd-medications

Understood Team. (n.d.-d). *How to talk to teens about adhd medication*. Understood. https://www.understood.org/en/articles/6-things-your-tween-or-teen-needs-to-understand-about-adhd-medication

u/rouditr. (2020). *Can the Flash Possibly Have ADHD*. https://www.reddit.com/r/DCcomics/comments/matg9s/discussion_can_the_flash_possible_have_adhd/

VanDuzer, T. (2020, October 23). *Time management techniques for teens: The ultimate guide*. Student-Tutor Education Blog. https://student-tutor.com/blog/time-management-techniques-for-teens/

Wheeler, R. B. (2022, August 25). *Communication hacks for adhd*. WebMD. https://www.webmd.com/add-adhd/adhd-communication-hacks

Willard, C. (2022, April 13). *Mindfulness exercises for teens with adhd: 6 easy strategies*. Additude. https://www.additudemag.com/slideshows/mindfulness-exercises-for-teens-adhd/

ABOUT THE AUTHOR

Leila Molaie holds a bachelor's degree in education, a Master of Science in Vocational Rehabilitation Counseling, and an Executive Master's in Rehabilitation Administration. For over thirteen years, she dedicated herself to educating high school students facing multiple challenges, recognizing their unlimited potential for success. Transitioning to the vocational rehabilitation field, she eagerly sought opportunities to integrate her teaching background with counseling skills. Throughout her career, she witnessed firsthand the profound impact of ADHD on young individuals' lives, observing their struggles in various aspects. Recognizing the lack of appropriate assistance, support, and education available to children and youth with ADHD, she was motivated to create a book that empowers parents and adolescents with practical strategies to manage ADHD and overcome life's obstacles.

This book draws inspiration from the author's decades of experience assisting children and teenagers with

ADHD. Its purpose is to encourage young readers to adopt a positive perspective and view their ADHD as an asset, unlocking the secrets to a fulfilling life while minimizing the adverse effects of ADHD symptoms.

By reading this book, you will gain valuable techniques for effectively managing ADHD symptoms during adolescence. You will also learn strategies to improve focus and achieve your goals successfully. The book supports parents of children and youth with ADHD, directly addressing adolescents as "you" to empower them and instill a sense of control over their lives. It explores what constitutes a successful and fulfilling life, even in the face of ADHD challenges. It guides readers to embrace their ADHD as a unique strength, becoming an asset to themselves and their families.

Throughout the book, numerous strategies, techniques, and guidelines are presented to allow readers to choose the best path suited to their circumstances. The author emphasizes that we are all unique and different from others in many ways, and a one-size-fits-all approach is not applicable.

Printed in Great Britain
by Amazon